Broken Wings

The Night the Cheering Stopped

Dave Schultz

with

Charlie Vincent

Cev Press
Grosse Pointe, MI

Broken Wings
Copyright © 1998 by Dave Schultz and Charlie Vincent
All rights reserved including the right of reproduction
in whole or in part in any form

Layout, design, & technical services by Matthew Gwinn

Back cover photo by Mary Schroeder / Detroit Free Press

Published by Cev Press
Grosse Pointe, MI

ISBN 1-891143-51-4

Printed in the United States of America

FOREWARD

It was the middle of a mid-November afternoon when I first heard the name: Dave Schultz.

I had kept up with the news about the limousine accident that almost cost Sergi Mnatsakanov and Vladimir Konstantinov their lives and took both a physical and mental toll on Slava Fetisov, a legitimate Russian hero. But mostly I read the names of the hockey players, the name of the guy who was driving that night -- Richard Gnida -- and the name of the limo company, which employed him.

When I heard Schultz's name the first time, I had no idea who he was. I didn't know he was the man who had spent two months trying to make sense of a senseless accident.

Like most Detroiters, I had been captivated with what the Red Wings did in the National Hockey League playoffs last Spring, with the way the Russians -- who once had been criticized as "too soft" -- became the core of the team that Scotty Bowman had built by bringing to Joe Louis Arena the best players not only from North America, but from Europe and the former Soviet Union too.

Their Stanley Cup victory had a galvanizing effect on southeast Michigan. Everyone identified with the Red Wings. Everyone felt a joy in what they had accomplished, but no one was really prepared for the outpouring of affection and admiration that a million fans rained down on them during their victory parade through downtown Detroit.

And, like most Detroiters, I remember where I was when I heard of the tragic accident that put a stop to the partying, put a stop to the celebration. I was watching TV, with my wife, when the network programming was interrupted to tell us about the accident, bringing us pictures of that crumpled up white limo wrapped around a tree in Birmingham. At first the details were sketchy, and as we would later learn, many of those early details also were not entirely accurate.

It was a front page story for a long time and I guess I had been as surprised as anyone that the case sort of seemed to play out with only a whimper, all the wind out of its sails. What had begun as such a loud, sensational, emotional story on the night of Friday, June 13, slipped quietly out of our consciousness in October, when Gnida was sentenced to nine months in jail for driving without a valid license.

A new hockey season was upon us. It was football season, too. And basketball season. And life went on.

The first time I heard Schultz's name was when Fred McLeod walked up to me in the small room at the Pistons' practice facility in Auburn Hills, where Doug Collins kept the media out of sight while the team was practicing -- far from the court so no prying eyes could see any of the secret things that were going on there.

"I've got to talk to you about something," McLeod said softly, flashing a piece of paper, with a few scribbled words on it, in my face.

We walked into a vacant office and McLeod, who telecasts Pistons games among his other many and varied television jobs in Detroit, told me he had recently made the acquaintance of a Birmingham cop.

This cop, McLeod said, was the guy who investigated the limousine accident. All of it. It was his investigation, if not exactly from the beginning, surely to the end.

"The guy wants to write a book about it," McLeod said.

"But he knows he can't do it by himself, and he asked me if I knew of anyone who might be interested in doing it with him. I told him I had a few thoughts, and you were one of them.

"Here's his name and address, if you want to call," and he slipped the piece of paper into my hand.

I am far from being an expert on hockey or on the Red Wings. The fall and winter are times I usually spend covering the Detroit Lions and Pistons, seldom the Red Wings. Others on our staff at the Free Press do that better than I could.

So I hesitated for a couple days.

I looked at the name and the phone number and wondered what I would be getting myself into, if I made the call. I wondered if it was worth the effort, worth the time.

But eventually I made the call and made arrangements to meet Schultz at his Bloomfield home.

He greeted me with a mountain of information, police records, memos, notes and diagrams, photos and sketches. He had kept a detailed file of his investigation and when he asked his superiors for permission to write about the accident, they gave him -- if not exactly their blessing, their approval.

Dave Schultz, it turned out, has been a cop half his life. He has done undercover work, been instrumental in drug busts, ticketed speeders, juggled paperwork, investigated high-profile cases like the Oakland County Rapist in the 1980s and the Oakland County Child Killer, in the late '70s. And last summer, he investigated the crash that stunned the city just six days after the Red Wings won the Stanley Cup championship.

From the first time I met him, one thing was obvious: This is a man who loves his job.

But, I wondered, who wants to read about the investigation?

Won't it be dull? Won't it be just statistics? Just black-and-white, ho-hum documentation of a car crash?

Coming from Dave Schultz's notes, and from his mouth, it was anything but dull.

Dave Schultz, besides being a career cop, is a lively storyteller.

His recollection of the investigation, of the interviews and the conversations, of the conflicts, the wild goose chases that got in the way and the final resolution of the case, entertained me for months. We hope it will inform and entertain you for a few hours.

This is his story, not mine.

He devoted a couple months to an investigation which often branched out into the most bizarre of possibilities, but always focused on one simple question: Why did the car driven by Richard Gnida hit that tree in the middle of Woodward just after 9:00 P.M., that Friday night?

In the end, he believes, he found the answers.

But his answers were never presented to a jury for a verdict.

This is the story of one cop's search for the truth and the sometimes-strange paths that search caused him to walk. It is a story filled with innuendos and accusations and threats, with leads that turn into deadends and an apparent deadend that gave Schultz the proof he felt he needed to charge Gnida with causing serious injury to his passengers that night in June.

But Richard Gnida went to jail because his license

was suspended, instead of being arraigned on any charge that might have explained why the limo went out of control, left the roadway and crashed.

It is a story that held Detroit, Michigan and much of the nation riveted last summer while Mnataskanov and Konstantinov fought for their lives. Today both of them are making steady, but slow, recoveries from their injuries; Fetisov, fully recovered from the injuries and nearing the end of his storied career, is trying to help the Red Wings to another Stanley Cup title; Gnida is well into his nine-month sentence and Dave Schultz is back to routine duty with the Birmingham Police Department.

And in the meantime, I've learned a lot about how a police investigation works and I've learned -- that if most of them are dull -- the investigation of the Red Wings' limo accident was an exception.

Charlie Vincent

Sergei Mnatsakanov -- six nights before the accident -- holds the Stanley Cup over his head as the Red Wings, including Steve Yzerman and Vladimir Konstantinov, celebrate their victory at Joe Louis Arena. (Bill Fundaro photo)

For Jared, Evan and Trevor

CHAPTER 1

Whatever the crisis, I didn't want any part of it.

The steaks were almost done, the children were in bed and finally, Kathy and I were going to enjoy an evening in our new home, after two months of commuting between Shelby Township, where our kids were finishing the 1997 school year, and Bloomfield, where our new home was within an easy drive of our work.

So when the telephone rang, we looked at each other and did not need to speak to know we had agreed not to answer. It was a little after 9 o'clock and phone calls at that time of night are almost always from work and this Friday -- Friday the 13th -- was not for work.

The commuting had been stressful, but two days earlier Shelby schools had let out for the summer and this weekend we would relax.

It would be the last relaxing one for a while, as it turned out.

I'd got off work at 2 o'clock and wasn't scheduled back in to the Birmingham Police Department until Sunday. Saturday was my day to watch our three children while Kathy worked at St. Joseph Mercy Hospital in Pontiac.

The night was for us.

We had the steaks, we had the rented video -- Absolute Power -- and we had each other. It was a night for us alone.

"Let somebody else handle it," I said, when the phone finally stopped ringing.

But in just a couple of minutes, my beeper went off. I'm not required to carry one in my job as accident investigator, but I choose to. I have a lot of things going on. It went off just as I walked onto the deck off the back of our house. And that's when I heard the sirens, too.

I mean a ton of 'em. All over the place.

Kathy and I looked at each other and I said: "Hey, I've already had a drink; forget it. Somebody else will handle it. They're all qualified."

But I knew by then that this was probably something serious, because it wouldn't normally be the telephone, the beeper and all of those sirens, all three.

"Somebody's in big trouble," I said. "It's probably fatal."

I've seen my share of things like that and been through a lot of different scenes in my 21 years of police work.

In the early '80s, I did undercover work that helped bust some drug dealers in Quarton Park. Fourteen people were arrested for possession and the sale of cocaine, marijuana, hashish, LSD and amphetamines.

I was young and excited about doing that kind of work. The undercover work in the park began because there had been some complaints from people who lived in the area, but it wasn't supposed to be anything like it turned out. I don't think anybody believed there was a major drug problem down there, but after spending a little time there it was obvious there was a lot of activity around.

The day after we made the bust, I go to the bar and everybody is saying, "Hey, you're famous" and "We saw you on TV" and all this and the next thing I know I get a call from the department and they tell me to call the FBI right away. I think they want one of my suspects to flip and all this kind of stuff. But they say, "Don't move! Stay right where you are, we'll be right there!"

Turns out they got information that there was a

murder contract on me for $55,000. They absolutely took it seriously and so did I. So they come and whisk me out of there and take me downtown and 24 hours later I've got a new identity and I'm gone.

I was sent out of town and did police work somewhere else -- I was single at the time. So three or four months later they said it was safe, that the contract was no longer out. But I stayed gone for about a year or so, because Traverse City is a great place to work.

I'd got into law enforcement for a couple of reasons; I had thought about it when I was in high school in Wyandotte, and when I got to college I heard, unlike business and pre-law, which was something else I'd thought about, I could get my grades up in a law enforcement course.

I went to Northwestern Michigan College, a two-year school in Traverse City, basically because my grades weren't good enough for a four-year school and because there was some money off tuition for playing basketball there.

After two years, when a lot of other people were switching to four-years schools, I had no money to switch and my parents couldn't give me money for college, so I decided: "Now's the time to go to work."

I remember sitting down with a Michigan map. I wanted to work Downriver or with the Wayne County Sheriff's Department, but I just needed a job quick and Birmingham was the first city to let me take the test and I got the job -- $17,500 starting partolman's pay in April of '77. It was my first job and I was making more money than my father, who had worked 35 years at the same chemical plant.

Since then, it's turned out to be a pretty wild career.

Once, after tesifying against a couple of guys in a drug case, a juror started choking on a piece of gum while they were deliberating. The people were frantic in there, they were yelling for somebody to help, so myself and David Lunsford, an investigator for the Oakland Prosecutors Office, went in and helped her. Her face was blue when we got there, but she came out of it OK.

The only problem was, after the jury found the defendants guilty, their attorney filed an appeal because we went into the jury room and the Appeals Court agreed with them that it might have prejudiced the jury, because we helped one of them out. So they threw out the conviction because they said, "entering a jury room is indefensible, no matter by whom."

I agreed with 'em. I knew it would be thrown out as soon as it happened. I mean, here's a cop saving a juror's life right in front of the other jurors, c'mon. I knew what would happen.

Eventually, though, they were retried and convicted.

There's been good things and bad along the way; I was named Birmingham Police Officer of the Year a couple of times, but on this Friday night I just wanted to be a citizen for a few hours. Everything had been so crazy with my life, with moving and everything, that I really didn't know if I wanted to get involved in something major at that point.

So we ate the steaks, had a couple of drinks, watched the video and went to bed.

Kathy was up at 4:30 Saturday morning to go to work and when I got up she had already seen the newspaper. The first thing she said to me was, "You're not going to believe this."

"The accident?"

And there it was on the front page.

But it wasn't even headlines, because Timothy McVeigh had been sentenced that day and that was the headline; on the side it was the Red Wings' accident and it said they were seriously injured. That was it, basically.

I'm not particularly a big hockey fan. I've only been to a couple of games, but of course, I knew who they were. I'm a newspaper junkie, so by reading so much about them I've always felt I knew as much as my buddies who went to games.

SATURDAY, JUNE 14 -- The Free Press' first reaction to the accident, because of the lateness of it -- and because of Timothy McVeigh's death sentence the same day -- was muted.

And, of course, the town hadn't been talking about much else since they won the Stanley Cup six days earlier.

TUESDAY, JUNE 10 -- Tuesday's parade drew more than a million to downtown Detroit and it seemed nothing could go wrong, nothing could spoil, what this hockey team had done. (Detroit Free Press)

As an investigator, I was curious, even though I wasn't working and at that point I had nothing to do with the case. So I called the dispatcher Saturday afternoon and asked if everything was going OK and was told nothing was happening.

Looking back, if our department made any mistakes -- and I don't know that it did -- it's that nothing got done that weekend, at all.

One thing was that the officer who answered the call on Friday night just did a search warrant to get blood from the driver -- at that time I didn't even know his name. I probably would have done the same thing. But in the end that caused some problems, because we probably should have got a urine sample, too.

It turns out that not just every lab can test blood for marijuana and before this investigation was through, that would become a very important point.

On the way to work Sunday morning, I drove by the accident site for the first time, with all the Teddy Bears and things under the tree that the limousine had hit and that's when I started to hear, "Hey, they're not going to make it."

Mark Rouland was the investigator who responded to the scene Friday night and, generally, it would have been his case from then on. As a matter of fact on Monday, the deputy chief, Richard Patterson, told me that was the case and that I was to assist him. But Mark is going through law school. On Monday morning, when we really started to get bombarded on this thing, swamped with calls and everything, Mark said he was wiped out and didn't want any part of what this was going to become. I can understand him making that decision. Law school was taking a lot of his time.

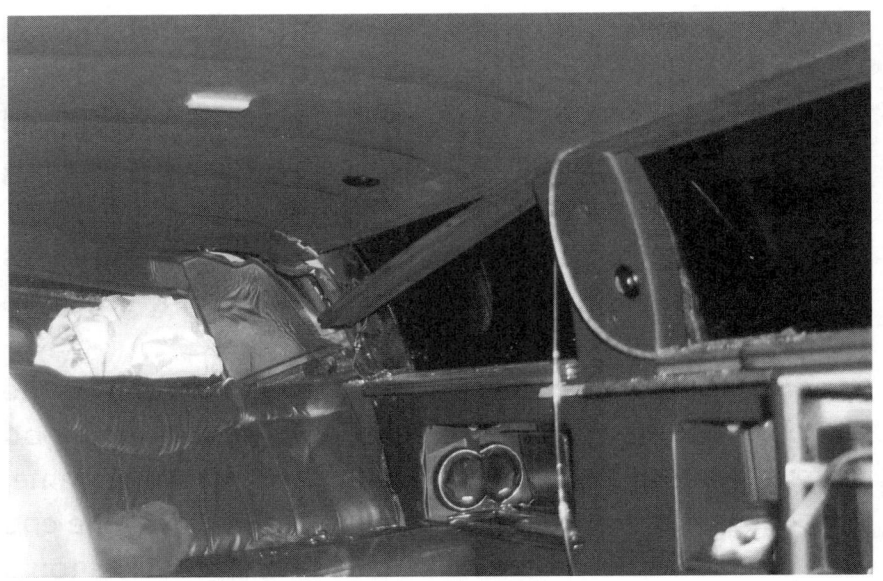

When the limo hit the tree in the median, Konstantinov, Mnatsakanov and Fetisov were thrown violently forward, slamming into the roof and the partition that separates the passenger's compartment from the driver. The force of their collision with the partition moved it forward about 18 inches. (Mark Rouland/Birmingham Police Department)

That's when Deputy Chief Patterson came to me and said somebody's got to do this.

By then it's pretty clear what we had here and I told him, "I'm not going to do this halfway...This is a big case. There's already some things that should have been done that haven't been done yet. We've got to do them now. If I'm going to be in charge, this is going to be my deal absolutely."

And he gave me full run. I was relieved of all my other duties.

The first thing we did was call for a drug dog from the Oak Park State State Police post before we did anything else with the vehicle on Monday.

The dog gave indications of possible traces of drugs but that would be true in just about any vehicle that's used to transport lots of people. There was no indication of any major drugs.

Next Larry Richardson, a state police accident reconstructionist who we'd used before, came over and we checked out the car, tore it apart and made sure the brakes were fine and checked the steering mechanism. Those were the two biggest things at that point, because we were looking for anything that might have caused the accident and we determined that everything was OK.

Richardson's exam, though, turned up something that demanded we make note of it. There was no evidence that the driver, at any time, used the brakes, so it seemed that probably the driver was not conscious even after the car went over the curb.

Evidence inside the limo gave us a pretty good idea what happened at impact. There was blood on the front windshield that indicated the driver had struck his head near the top of the roofline.

In the passengers' compartment, there was a white smear near the end of the bar. The divider, between the driver and the passengers, was pushed approximately 18 inches towards the driver's compartment, from the impact of the players hitting it. Hair samples were imbedded in the divider and in the roof and we made note that there were several pieces of broken glass, covered with blood.

When I got back to the station, I started going over reports from the accident scene and witness statements.

Tim Exleby was the first officer from our department on the scene.

His report noted:

"Dispatched to the area of 16 Mile and Woodward to check on a reported Personal Injury involving a limo.

Upon arrival I observed a white limo in the median between southbound and northbound Woodward near Redding. Limo had heavy front end damage from making contact with a tree in the median.

Officers Steve Alexander and Scott Wilson from Bloomfield Hills P.D. arrived at the same time. I approached the driver side of the vehicle and observed a white male sitting on the ground leaning against the limo. Subject was bleeding from the mouth and nose. I asked him if he was OK and he stated he was. I asked him if he was the driver and he stated he was.

"I then went to the driver side area of the limo and observed a white male (Vladimir Konstantinov) lying on his back outside the vehicle and his feet were still inside the vehicle. Subject had a bad gash on the left side of his face and appeared to be unconscious. Subject also appeared to be having trouble breathing. There were two citizens at the scene who were with the subject keeping

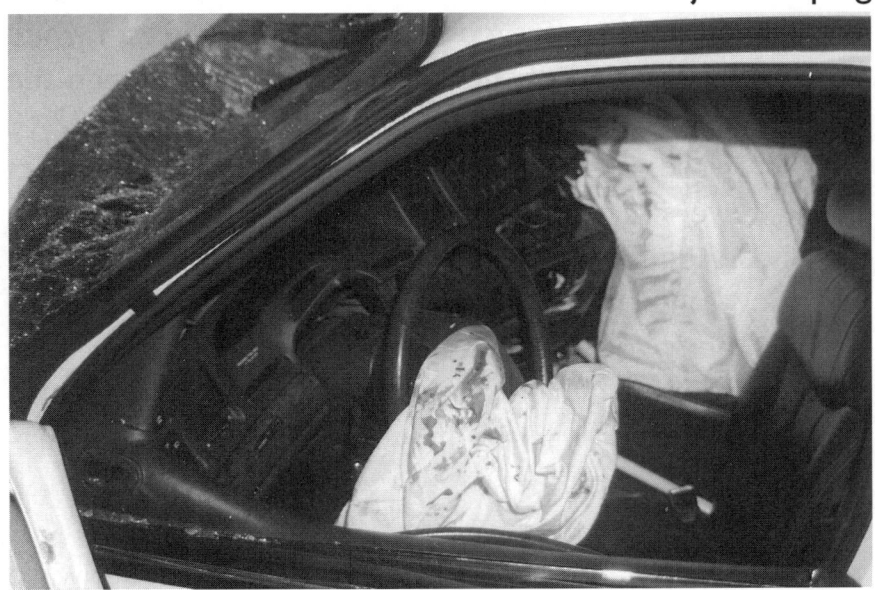

Inside the driver's compartment of the Gambino limousine shows driver Richard Gnida's blood on the air bags. (Mark Rouland/Birmingham Police Department)

BIRMINGHAM POLICE DEPT.
151 Martin Street, P.O. Box 3001, Birmingham, MI 48012
Phone: (810) 644-3405 ORI-MI632-5900

NARRATIVE REPORT PAGE 8 OF 10   ☐ SUPP ☐ CORR ☐ DELETE

DATE	DAY	SHIFT	PLATOON	BADGE 1	BADGE 2	INCIDENT	CLR ARREST	UNF	PRIM CLASS		INCIDENT NUMBER
06,13,97	Fri	0.3	02	024		STATUS ☐ CLR EXCEPT ☐ INACT			3125		

01
02 w/m (Monzaconoff) that was lying on his back inside the limo. The
03 subj. had a severe head injury and I noticed some brain matter on
04 the subj left side of his head. The doctors were just holding the
05 subj. head still until EMS arrived with neck braces and back
06 boards.
07   I radioed to dispatch and advised them that we would need an
08 accident investigator and some supervisors at the scene. EMS
09 arrived shortly after.
10   After everyone was being tended to I went back to the driver
11 and asked him what had happened. He stated he remembered coming s/b
12 on Woodward and the lane in front of him was clear. He states he
13 then remembers striking the curb and going up onto the median.
14 Driver says he tried swerving to avoid the other obstacles in the
15 roadway and suddenly struck the tree.
16   I asked the driver if he was cut off and he stated he was not.
17 I asked him if there were any veh around him and he stated there
18 was not. I then asked him why he went up onto the median and he
19 stated he didn't know why. Driver thinks he blacked out. He
20 remembers the roadway being clear in front of him and then
21 remembers striking the curb. He doesn't remember between the two
22 incidents.
23   I asked the driver if he had anything to drink and he stated
24 he did not. I again asked him if he had anything at all and he
25 stated, "not today.". I pressed the subj. to be truthful with me
26 and to tell me if he anything earlier in the day that would cause
27 this accident and he stated a third time that he had nothing.

INVESTIGATING OFFICER(S): Tim C. REVIEWED BY: RW   ASSIGNED TO/BADGE: ATTENTION TO:

A portion of the narrative report, written by Tim Exelby on the night of the accident notes the apparent severity of the injury to Sergei Mnatsakanov and Richard Gnida's vague recollection of what happened.

The initial accident report. Someone at the station noted that the accident on Friday the 13th; we received the call at 13 minutes after 9 o'clock and that the case number was 97-9513.

his head immobilized and keeping his airway clear.

"I went to the passenger side of the vehicle where officers Wilson and Alexander were attending to a white male (Fetisov) that was lying on the ground outside the vehicle. Subject had severe gashes to his legs and also appeared to be unconscious.

"I then stepped inside the limo...and observed two doctors that stopped to assist with the accident. They were attending to a white male (Monzaconoff) that was lying on his back inside the limo. The Subject had a severe head injury and I noticed some brain matter on the subj left side of his head. The doctors were just holding the subj head still until EMS arrived with neck braces and back boards. I radioed to dispatch and advised them that we would need an accident investigator and some supervisors on the scene...after everyone was attended to, I went back to the driver and asked him what had happened. He stated he remembered coming s/b on Woodward and the lane in front of him was clear. He states he then remembers striking the curb and going up onto the median. Driver says he tried swerving to avoid the other obstacles in the roadway and suddenly struck the tree.

"I asked the driver if he was cut off and he stated he was not. I asked him if there were any veh around him and he stated there was not. I then asked him why he went up on the median and he stated he didn't know why. Driver thinks he blacked out. He remembers the roadway being clear in front of him and then remembers striking the curb. He doesn't remember between the two incidents.

"I asked the driver if he had anything to drink and he stated he did not. I again asked him if he had anything at all and he stated, 'not today.' I pressed the subj. to be truthful

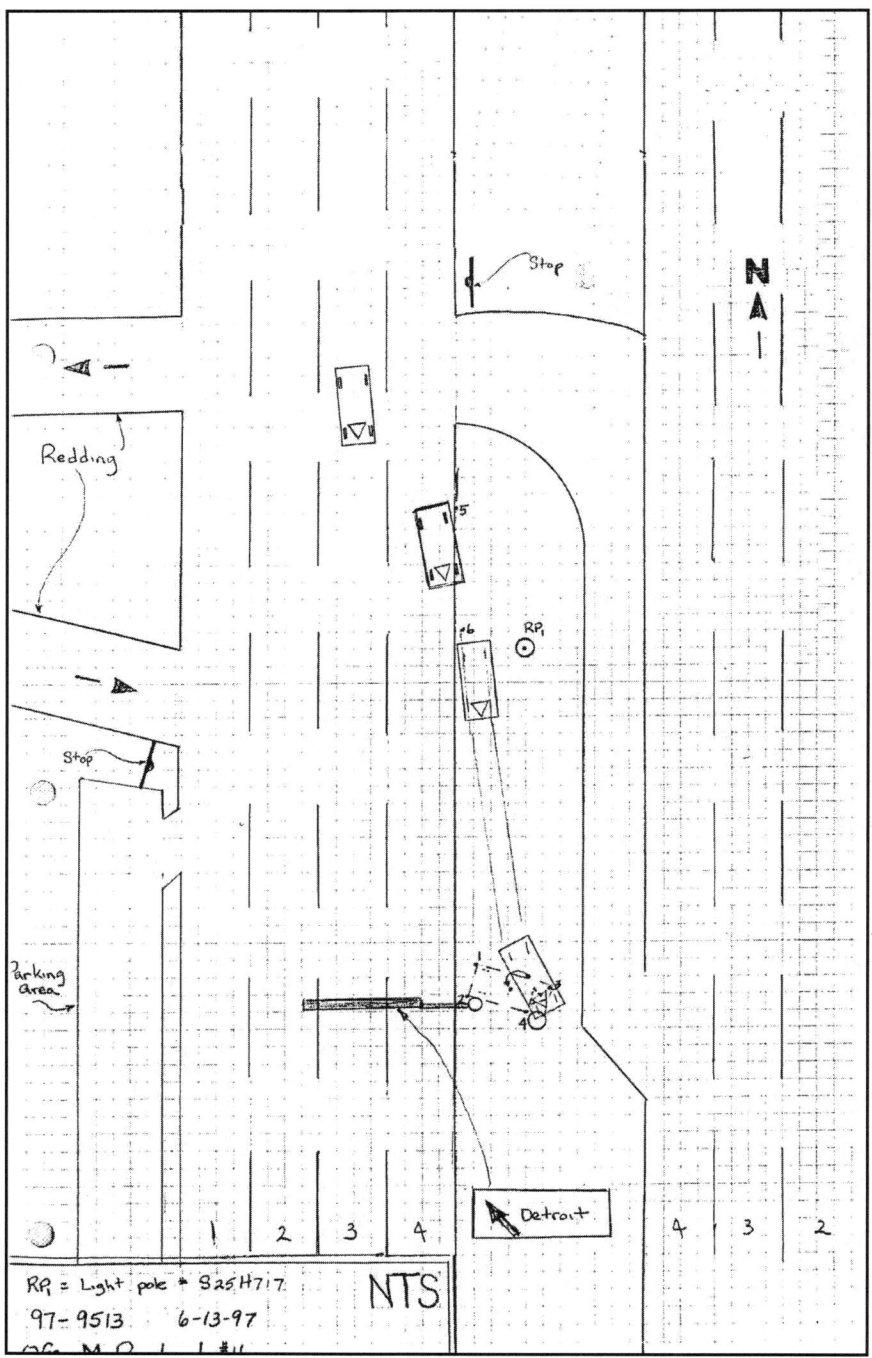

Officer Mark Rouland made this sketch of the limousine's path from the point it began to veer out of control, until it collided with the tree, sending the rear of the car around to hit the sign pole.

When we conducted the tests of the accident site on Monday these photos were taken to illustrate where the car left the roadway and jumped onto the median, and to show the damage to the tree Gnida hit. (Ofc. Mark Rouland Photos)

with me and to tell me if he (drank) anything earlier in the day that would cause this accident and he stated a third time that he had nothing.

"While talking with the driver I noticed his eyes were glassy and that his speech was slurred. (also noticed nose and mouth damage.) There was an odor of alcohol in the air but it seemed to be coming from inside the vehicle. I looked inside the driver side window and noticed a water bottle on the driver side of the limo. I then went into the back of the veh and noticed several glasses inside the vehicle along with the strong odor of alcohol. There was liquid all over the inside of the limo that appeared and smelled like intoxicants.

"Occupants of the limo were transported to Beaumont. Scene was turned over to Officer Rouland and MSP to record and log...Sgt. Schettenhelm and Cpl. Manigold...advised me to seek a warrant on the drivers blood due to the nature of the injuries to the passengers in the limo. Warrant was drawn up by ofc. and signed by Judge Small of the 48th district court.

"LEIN (Law Enforcement Information Network) shows the driver to be suspended UDR at the time of the accident. Subject has two prior drunk driving convictions."

Rouland's report from the night concluded: "Based on the witness statements and physical evidence so far, it appears that at the time of the accident, that the limo driver was southbound on Woodward in the #3 lane. It drifted to the #4 lane, then struck the median curb. The car skidded on the curb for some distance before finally entering the median grass. The car continued without slowing significantly until it struck a tree. At that point, the back of the car spun to the west and struck a sign post. The car came to a rest at that point. Unknown persons then removed Konstantinov and Fetisov from the car and placed them on the ground. It does not appear that any of the passengers were ejected from the car."

As the investigation went on, we would discover that the three passengers, Vladimir Konstantinov, Sergei Mnatsakanov and Slava Fetisov -- who six days earlier had helped bring the Stanley Cup to Detroit -- screamed to the driver when they felt the car veer towards the median, that they shouted and that what they did then may have accounted for why Konstantinov and Mnatskanov were seriously injured and Fetisov was not.

Much later, too, we would find out that the first people on the scene were Richard Harrison, a 55-year-old insurance salesman, and Karen McTaggert, and aerobics instructor and human resources specialist. They had heard the sound of the crash while having dinner.

"I looked out and saw it and told her to call 911, and I got right over there and there were others coming, too, from all over. The first thing I saw was that the driver was making the most noise. He was yelling that he was on fire. Everybody else was unconscious," Harrison recalled.

"There were fluids from the car dripping on the driver but there was no fire, but still, he was screaming: 'I'm on fire! I'm on fire! Help me!'

"I told him to be calm and to power his window down, but it didn't work, so then I told him to cover up as much as he could and be calm, that I was going to break the window and he just started screaming: 'No! No!'

"The driver's side door was sort of ajar and I wrapped my leather jacket over it and kneed the glass out. There was still some jagged glass in there and I really couldn't get him through there, so I reached up and pulled the rest of the door frame down. I don't know how I did it; I probably couldn't do it again.

"Once I got him outside, I had him leaning against the vehicle and he told me he was OK, but he was really hyper. He kept getting up, like a child. I kept telling him to sit down, but he didn't stay."

Confident the driver was not seriously injured, Harrison went to the back of the limo, where one passenger was laying, partially out of the vehicle.

"I looked inside and could see there was another person in there who needed help, his legs were jerking back and forth, back and forth. I could tell he had gone through the bar, hit the divider and then come back through the bar again and tore himself all up. I tried to comfort him, but I knew better than to touch him or move him at all.

"I stayed right with him until a doctor showed up.

Richard Gnida (in tux at right) sits on the ground after the accident, while others work on the injured Red Wings. (Stuart Laidlaw photo)

The most important thing I did after that, I guess, was get a policeman to give us a flashlight while they did work on him and eventually we inched him onto a backboard, one of us taking his feet, another his midsection and another his head. We inched him onto the board and we inched the board out the door.

"When we got him out, I saw Karen was working with another injured person on the ground and everything seemed to be beyond what I could do anymore about so I went home. I had done all I could do and I didn't care to stay around for any 'Atta Boys'.

"It wasn't until we were watching TV a little later that night that we learned who the injured people were."

That was the clearest and most detailed picture of what happened in the first minutes after the accident, but I didn't hear it until much later.

Now -- three days after the accident that shook metropolitan Detroit to its core -- we knew hardly anything.

One thing we did know, though, was that we had a problem with the fans who wanted to congregate at the accident site. It wasn't a problem as far as rowdiness; the people who were there were very respectful. A couple of neighbors didn't like it, but the people out there weren't drinking and having a party and all that. The problem was, it was such a major road and all the gawkers were stopping and slowing down and we got several accidents out there.

From a public relations aspect it was like: what do we do here? A number one, it's not like they were creating a problem. Nobody thought they were, but we knew if we shut it down, we're going to look like the biggest meanies in the world.

But when there was an injury accident out there Monday night, we decided to shut it down and what was amazing was the people understood and the news media, instead of saying we were the Gestapo, throwing everyone out, actually handled it pretty good.

We loaded up all the Teddy Bears and everything that had been left at the site and took them to Joe Louis and dropped them off with the Wings. We'd already taken them a golf bag and clubs, a couple sleeves of balls, some candy, golf towels and three jerseys -- two home and one away -- that were in the trunk of the limo.

About 6 o'clock Tuesday morning we met and went to the site and, with a bunch of cones, closed down Woodward so we could reconstruct what had happened.

Usually, from an investigative point of view, you can determine what happened, just by what's left. In 90 per-

Almost as soon as the limousine was towed away, Red Wing fans turned the accident site into a shrine in honor of the injured players. (Stuart Laidlaw photo)

Fans brought balloons, signs, ribbons, flowers, Teddy Bears, everything you could think of to mark the spot where the accident happened and they didn't stop, even when we forced them to move to a different location because of the danger of being in the center of the median. (Stuart Laidlaw photo)

Fans respond to the accident by signing a giant Get Well card in Birmingham (Richard Lee/Detroit Free Press)

cent of the accidents, the marks left on the road, the skid marks and the damage to the vehicle will tell you a story itself.

Here there were no skid marks whatsoever, even without the witness statements, with no skid marks, no yaw marks, that would completely rule out any kind of evasive movement. If you turn your car to avoid somebody, you're going to leave marks. Here, there's nothing. I mean, zero.

The only actual mark that vehicle left, outside of what happened to the tree, is you could see where it hit the curb. A mark from the rim, along the curb.

We ruled out any kind of evasive action and put the speed at no more than 50 miles per hour and the limit there is 45. If he was over the limit, it wasn't by much.

By reconstructing where the car was when it began to veer, his speed and the distance to the tree, we figured the whole thing -- from the time the players noticed something was wrong, until impact -- took eight seconds.

I came away from there knowing, right off the bat that the accident reconstruction wasn't going to tell us anything outside of that and the fact he didn't evade anything and he wasn't really going over the speed limit.

There was nothing there.

Because of a lack of skid marks and the driver's original statement, that he thought he'd blacked out, we figured the guy wasn't conscious when this happened. But we didn't know why he wasn't conscious.

I went back to the department and looked up Deputy Chief Patterson.

"This is going to be one long investigation," I said.

CHAPTER 2

By Tuesday afternoon, we'd gathered some information on Richard Gnida; we knew about his driving record and we were ready to talk to him.

His driving record was awful.

He was arrested for driving while impaired in May of 1994, behind the wheel of a Gambino limo. They had to tow the car away.

In February of 1996, he was pulled over in Adrian -- driving a Gambino car again -- for speeding and when it turned out his license was suspended, he was arrested. Another driver, who was following him, Dawn Council, had to stay with the two cars until another driver was brought out to pick up Gnida's.

His license had been revoked just a month earlier.

```
Photo#:    16000524
Inc #:     979513
Last:      GNIDA
First:     RICHARD
Middle:    ALAN
Arr Date:  10/02/1997
DOB:       07/31/1969
Sex:       MALE
Race:      WHITE
Height:    600
Weight:    180
Jewelery:
```

Richard Gnida's Birmingham Police Department Mug shot; I couldn't believe how frail and scared he looked the first time I saw him.

So you wonder what is a guy thinking, with a record like that, getting behind the wheel of a car, with other people's lives in his hands?

He hadn't been wearing a seatbelt at the time of the accident, but the airbag had saved him from any injury other than the bump to the head, when he hit the roof, just over the steering wheel.

The toxicology report from the hospital showed no drugs in his body, no alcohol, only nicotine. But the screen that a hospital does in a case like that is just a quick screen to make sure a patient doesn't need to be detoxed right away.

The question we all had at that point -- and in fact, through the entire investigation -- was: What made him run off the road and into that tree?

When he comes in to talk to me, I'm looking for A number one, what he did. There are things I haven't ruled out. I, from right off the bat, sincerely believe he did not fall asleep. I have firm opinions on that and I don't believe it's possible. I don't believe it's an option; I believe something else happened.

It could have been several things.

Alcohol. But then I believed what the hospital was saying.

Drugs, either that he took intentionally or that he took, maybe, unintentionally.

Medication.

Or the option that he had a medical condition.

I've had cases where a guy had a seizure or something like that, and I had a very open mind on that matter.

We were anxious, or course, to talk to him and we set up a meeting in Deputy Chief Patterson's office. I asked if he wanted to sit in on it, but he said: "No, it's your baby, just keep me appraised of what's going on."

I'd asked the Oakland County Prosecutor's office if they wanted to sit in, too. That's pretty much protocol, but they chose not to get involved at that point.

Gnida came in with his attorney, James O'Connell. Somehow they had slipped past the news media who were camped outside and after we said hello and things like that, we kind of got a laugh together about them being able to slip in, even though he should have been pretty obvious, since he was wearing a neck brace.

"How are you doing?" I asked.

"OK, just sore," Gnida said.

"What's the problem?"

"Strained ligaments."

I expected there would be some questions he would not answer, but when that happens, you try to go around a different way, if his attorney objects, and go in another direction. So I was prepared.

I asked if they were ready to get started and the both kind of nodded.

"What's your name?"

"Richard Alan Gnida."

"Your date of birth?"

"July 31, 1969."

And that's when his attorney stood up and said, "that's all the information you're getting..my client will not answer any more questions."

I was flabbergasted. A number one, because of the accident itself, I could see him getting to a point where he did not want to talk about it, but it was beneficial for him to give us some sort of statement.

I tried to get around their objections. I told them that we could talk about what had happened previous to the accident, what he did that day, what he did the day before. I told them we were looking at the possibility of fatigue being a factor, or we could talk about what happened on the golf course.

At every suggestion O'Connell said, "No."

I would eventually learn more about him and come not to trust him. Back in 1976 he had been convicted of conspiracy to break and enter and receiving stolen property -- some rare coins. The Appeals Court, though, later overturned his conviction, clearing him of any guilt. He had served as a municipal judge in Highland Park and, as an attorney, had been involved in some high-profile cases, maybe the highest profiled one was in 1991 when he defended Michael Cato, who was convicted of the ambush slaying of his brother-in-law, Anthony Riggs, right after Riggs came back from Operation Dessert Storm. That was the case where Cato's sister, Toni Cato Riggs, was also accused.

Anyway, once I got over being flabbergasted, which was pretty quick, I was mad. I mean, it was Gnida's right not to talk, but I wasn't happy with the way it was done and I didn't think he was getting good advise.

So I turned to him and said: "If you decide you want to talk to me, if you ever want to give your side of the story, please come in, feel free to come and talk to me."

He said, "OK." That's the only thing he said after giving me his name and birth date.

O'Connell was not pleased that I told him he could come in any time.

He said, "He's not going to talk with you."

"That's his right, too. But he can, if he wants to."

That was the first time I had met Gnida, and the thing that struck me was he was such a quiet guy, a hard guy to totally dislike, because he was kind of pathetic.

My first impression was that he looked sickly, how frail he was at that point and he also looked like a scared kid. He was almost petrified, you could tell just by looking at his face.

The whole interview lasted maybe ten minutes, with me sitting in the big chair behind Deputy Chief Patterson's chair and them sitting across from me.

I told Gnida just to make sure he didn't leave town, because I might be wanting to talk to him, that he didn't have to talk to the media, but at some point, he would have to talk with me.

And they took off.

*   *   *

At that point in time, we thought we might have one, maybe two, fatalities. That was the indication we got, both from talking to the people at the hospital and from talking to people around the Red Wings, so we knew we had to be real thorough on this.

And that made the only other person who could talk about what happened inside the limo -- Slava Fetisov -- a priority, someone we definitely wanted to talk to as soon as possible.

The first time we tried, Monday after the accident, it was a real madhouse around the hospital.

Two fans had somehow gotten into Mnatsakanov's room and when security discovered that, they really went ape. The people didn't do anything, but you can imagine

MONDAY, JUNE 16 -- The Wings were in everyone's prayers (Detroit Free Press)

the reaction to them just walking in there.

The hospital had given us the OK to talk to Fetisov, they said he was well enough for us to do that. Carole Ilitch-Trepeck said she had spoken to him and that he understood why we needed to talk to him.

He was aware of all the rumors out there and all the talk about the accident. One television station had reported Friday night that Mnatskanov had been killed in the accident.

There had been rumors that some of them had been thrown from the limo and talk that Fetisov was sitting by the window that divided the back part of the limo from the driver's portion and that that was why he wasn't hurt so badly.

If he had been up there, trying to shake the driver

awake -- as some of the rumors indicated -- that was very important. And because I was hearing it from so many places, I thought it was true.

Carole told me that's not what he told her, but I said, "OK, but I've still got to talk to him; I've still got to hear it from his own lips."

When I saw him for the first time, on Monday, you could tell he was very upset. He knew the other two guys were badly hurt. He was propped up in his bed and there was an attorney there, but he didn't say anything; he just stood in the background.

The only other people in the room were Larry Richardson from the state police, Carole, and her sister, Denise Ilitch-Lites, who was already in the room when we arrived.

Slava Fetisov (left) holds Stanley Cup and fellow Russian Igor Larinov skates beside him in victory celebration on the Saturday before the Friday the 13th accident. (Bill Fondaro Photo)

Fetisov says Wings tried to wake driver

Richard Gnida: "I might have blanked out," he told police.

Vigils continue as 2 patients remain critical

BY JASON LA CANFORA
AND BRIAN MURPHY
Free Press Staff Writers

Frantic screams suddenly filled the white stretch limousine Friday night when Red Wings Vladimir Konstantinov and Slava Fetisov and a team masseur noticed that their driver appeared to have dozed off at the wheel, according to people who have spoken with Fetisov in recent days.

Within moments, the car veered toward a Woodward median near Big Beaver Road, jumped a six-inch curb and smashed into a tree, turning a giddy weeklong Stanley Cup celebration into a heart-wrenching vigil for the injured players and masseur Sergei Mnatsakanov.

"I might have blanked out," 27-year-old driver Richard Gnida told police officers at the scene, according to Birmingham Deputy Police Chief Richard Patterson.

Gnida will be charged with driving with a suspended license, a misdemeanor punishable by up to 90 days in jail, Patterson said.

The possibility of more serious charges exists, but Patterson said the investigation is not complete and the findings must be reviewed by the Oakland County Prosecutor's Office.

Konstantinov and Mnatsakanov re-

Top: Wings coach Scotty Bowman looks at reporters as they question doctors at Beaumont. Above: Meagan Hallo takes a look at a rock in Chelsea recently painted with a message to honor if the injured Red Wings.

mained on ventilators Monday in critical condition — spending their third day in a coma at William Beaumont Hospital in Royal Oak.

With chest and lung injuries, Fetisov was the least seriously hurt, and is expected to be released from the hospital soon.

Although doctors said Monday that Fetisov, 39, did not remember the accident, he has recounted to members of the Wings organization and his family events leading up to the crash in Birmingham.

Some of those he spoke with shared his story with the Free Press.

Fetisov's recollections are the first account of what happened inside the car.

He said he was seated behind the driver, facing Konstantinov and Mnatsa-

Please see CRASH, Page 9A

MORE INSIDE

THE INJURIES: Updating the Wings' conditions. And a look at head injuries, a leading cause of death. 8A.

TWO SURVIVORS: The stories of two metro Detroiters show how widely head injury problems can vary. 8A.

A QUESTION OF SAFETY: Limo drivers say they all feel like suspects now. What laws cover them? 9A.

GET TOUGH: Limo regulations need tightening. 10A.

SOMBER CELEBRATION: Thursday's NHL awards show is sure to be dulled by Konstantinov's absence. 6C.

OUT OF FOCUS: TV coverage of the accident Friday night was less than stellar. 1D.

TUESDAY, JUNE 17 -- Fetisov's story, still dotted with as much rumor as fact, began to find its way into the newspaper by word of mouth from family and friends, even before I had held my interview with him.

We made a little small talk introduced each other all around and we shook hands and I told him: "I want to talk to you. I need to ask a couple of questions."

"I know that," Fetisov said.

"Officer Schultz, I will tell you exactly what happened, 100 percent. But I want to make sure it comes out right."

He told me he wanted his attorney to be there and he wanted an interpreter and as soon as they could get there from New York, he would talk to us.

He speaks English very well, but he was aware of what had gone out on the radio and television and in the newspapers that was not true and he was concerned that the things he said were interpreted by someone who has a better command of the English language than he does.

Richardson wanted to press him to talk then, just to give us some routine information. And he held a piece of paper out to Fetisov and said, "just draw us a diagram of where you were all sitting."

That's when Denise kind of stepped in and said we would have to wait, that he wasn't going to get into that then, and I agreed 100 percent. I didn't want to push it at that point.

I know athletes can sometimes be suspicious of police; they have their media image to keep up and I didn't want to get into a situation where the Wings would come out and say, "Nobody's going to talk to the police." It certainly didn't turn out that way; they cooperated straight through.

When we left Fetisov's room, Carole gave me a reason for Fetisov wanting to be so careful about making sure things he said were interpreted precisely. From talking to her, I came to understand how political he is in Russia --

and that led us down another road later, too. He wasn't the first Russian athlete to defect; he was the one who challenged the system and gained permission from the government to play in the NHL. To some back in Russia, he is looked upon as more than just a hockey player. He is looked upon as a hero and possibly there's a political career in his future when he's finished playing hockey.

So Wednesday morning -- after the disappointing meeting with Gnida on Tuesday -- we were back in Fetisov's room, with his agent-attorney, William Dowling, and Vladimar Zlobinsky, from Dowling's office, who was there to interpret.

Dowling, Zlobinsky, Carole Ilitch, Richardson and I had discussed the things we would cover, before we went in. I said: "All's I want to know is what happened from the time he got picked up that day, until the time of the accident."

Just to reassure them I had no interest in anything except the accident, I told then: "I don't care if they had 15 hookers out there at that place and I don't care if they drank a pint of tequila each." Obviously, we had no idea anything like that went on, I just wanted them to understand we didn't care about anything that didn't have anything to do with the accident.

Fetisov didn't want the interview taped and I didn't press it. I could understand that. He wasn't a suspect of any sorts and if I was in his shoes, I wouldn't want it taped, either. The next thing you know, your police interview's on some radio station.

When we walked into the room, he looked much better than he had two days before.

He seemed more comfortable, and even though the

interpreter was there, only a few words of Russian were spoken. A couple of times, I would ask a question and he would turn and answer to Zlobinsky in English and Zlobinsky would say, "this is what he means..."

His interest was just in making sure it came out in the right English words. His answers were in English with a Russian accent. Zlobinsky was very articulate, he added the "thes" and the "ands".

He told me that they all arrived at Chris Osgood's between two and three o'clock Friday afternoon. All week, Osgood's house was the center of Red Wings' activity. He lives in Birmingham, only about ten blocks from the station and they were just out there being guys.

Some of our guys got calls about loud parties, because that's were they'd start the night. But there was never any trouble there. Every night there was something planned, mostly official Red Wing functions and they'd end up back at Chris' house afterwards, too.

They'd been partying a lot around town, a lot of 'em showed up quite a bit at Dick O'Dow's, a bar in town.

Friday night was the first night when there was no official Red Wing function and since a lot of them were going to split over the weekend, they had scheduled a golf outing at The Orchards. Kris Draper set it up, they were just going to go out, play golf and have dinner and stuff, maybe play some cards, just an informal end to it all before they kind of broke up for the summer.

They basically all came out of the house at the same time and got into five limousines that were parked in front. They weren't assigned or anything. Guys just got into whichever one they chose.

Fetisov, Konstantinov and Mnatsakanov slid into the

passenger compartment of the limo driven by Richard Gnida.

Shortly after they left the subdivision and got out onto the main road, Fetisov said Konstantinov started complaining about the way the driver was driving, not necessarily the speed, but making turns from the wrong lane, in and out of traffic, the car jerking around the whole time.

Fetisov said the driving was bad but that Konstantinov was really complaining, making a really big thing out of it.

They made one stop on the way out to the golf course, to pick up cigars.

But once they were there, the Russians were not really into the golf aspect of things. Fetisov had an interview scheduled with a Russian newspaper reporter and the three of them decided they wanted to leave, before the golfing was over.

They'd all put up money for the closest to the pin and things like that, that golfers bet on and when they decided they were going to leave early, they asked Draper if they could get their money back and he told them that was OK with him, but they needed to see John Wharton, the Wings' trainer, because he was holding the money.

Fetisov said they found Wharton and told him what Draper had said and got their money back and were ready to leave, but when they got back to where the limos were parked, their driver wasn't there.

The irony is, they did not have assigned drivers, and could have taken any of the limos back to Birmingham, but apparently none of the other drivers volunteered to take them, so Konstantinov went looking for Gnida.

Brendon Shanahan, who wasn't golfing, showed up around that time and Fetisov and Mnatsakanov hung around and talked to him while Konstantinov was looking all over for their driver.

Fetisov said it took Konstantinov 20 to 30 minutes to find Gnida, who apparently had been off by himself, somewhere.

And when Konstantinov came back with him, Gnida had to ask another driver how to get back to Birmingham and that really set off Konstantinov again.

He's concerned now.

We even heard a rumor that Mike Vernon almost had to grab him by the seat of his pants and put him in the car, saying "everything's going to be OK." But that turned out not to be the case.

As nearly as we can tell, they left the golf course at 8:45.

I brought up the question of where he was sitting. I told him: "I heard that you were up in the front and trying to wake the driver up."

Fetisov said, "No...but I wish I would have. I wish I could have."

The window between the passenger compartment and the driver was open because Konstantinov had been up there -- more than once -- to check on the directions.

He was still concerned.

Fetisov was on the back seat, on the passenger's side, with his feet up on the bar. Mnatsakanov was directly across from him, on the left side of the back seat, and Konstantinov -- when he wasn't scooting up to make sure Gnida knew where he was going -- was on the seat on the left side of the limo, facing across it, towards the bar where Fetisov had his feet propped.

They probably all had drinks in their hands, and that's

After the Wings and Gnida were taken to the hospital and the crowd was cleared away, this is the way the accident site looked from every angle. Note the top half of the driver's side door is bent down; Richard Harrison, one of the first citizens on the scene, did that with his bare hands to free Gnida. (Mark Rouland/Birmingham Police Department)

absolutely OK. They had won the Stanley Cup. They were probably sitting back there, you know, saying, "God bless America!", "This is a great country!" or whatever.

None of them had on seat belts.

The last time Konstantinov slid up to check on Gnida, Fetisov said, was coming down Woodward, shortly before they crossed Big Beaver. He told Gnida to make sure he didn't go down Hunter, but that he took Woodward into downtown Birmingham.

Then Fetisov says, "I was looking through the window, watching to see that he was going to go into downtown Birmingham.

"We were in the right hand lane and there was nothing in front of us, whatsoever, and all of a sudden the car swerved, not evasive, just started drifting and immediately, as soon as it crossed one lane, all three of us started yelling: 'Hey, what's going on! Hey! Hey!'

"Officer Schultz, we hit the curb, then I see pole, then I see Mom, then I see Dad..."

I'll never forget the way he said that. He went on to name about three or four other friends who he saw -- all in an instant.

"Then we miss pole," Fetisov said. "Then there's a big, loud bang, then I wake up and I'm on top of Sergi and Vladdie. Then someone pull me out of the car."

You hear all the time about a person's life passing before their eyes, but here's someone from a foreign country, who just humanly tells you what he saw and you're talking about a time frame of only a few seconds and the description of what he saw seems like it would take ten minutes to go though his mind.

I never disbelieved those things happened, but I was

somewhat skeptical. I'm 100 percent a believer in that now.

Fetisov was probably unconscious just a moment, but he was confused after the wreck, and obviously concerned and not at all sure what had happened. He didn't know who was around and for whatever reason, he told me that when someone asked his name, he gave a different name than his own.

He was laying on the ground, face down, and he could see under the car. The people there told him not to move, but he said when they pulled Konstantinov out and laid him on the ground on the other side of the car he could see him.

He said he could see how bad "my buddy was hurt."

And Slava Fetisov, 39-years-old and so far from all that was familiar, his dream season suddenly not nearly as important as what had happened in an instant, began crying and could not stop.

CHAPTER 3

We were working with the Oakland County Prosecutors office on this by Wednesday -- five days after the accident, talking mostly to Jason Pernick, who is the chief of Warrants, and James Halushka. What I'm hearing from them is that, even without the toxicology reports, they were looking to charge Gnida with Felonious Driving.

Their thinking is that they had a tragic accident here and they're going to charge this guy to high heaven. I understood they felt what he had done was disregard for the life and safety of others, since he didn't have a license and all that.

If he had been a normal, 100-percent licensed driver, legal and fell asleep behind the wheel -- this was their philosophy -- he would have been charged with basic careless or a minor deal. But this was a guy that shouldn't have even been driving and knew it.

I just wanted to know what really happened and the investigation was totally in my hands.

I called them for direction and to keep them informed, but they just said, "Do your investigation and let us know what's going on." Their feeling was that if everything came back 100-percent negative for any kind of alcohol, drugs, whatever, they were still looking at the fact Gnida was not a licensed driver and they were going to pursue this.

He had a previous history of drinking and driving and they were big into charging him with something.

And it's fair to say I was suspicious, especially after talking to Fetisov. I mean these Russian hockey players are such loud voiced people, I was convinced Gnida was not just sleeping at the wheel. I've been an officer on midnights and I know how tired you can get. Nodding off, that can happen. But I don't believe it could happen over the length of time this took, with the movement that happened, with three loud guys yelling at you.

When we recreated the accident, starting from where the limo began to drift, until it hit the tree, we calculated the whole thing took eight seconds.

Eight seconds!

It doesn't sound like much, but that is a lot of time when you think about it.

You could read this paragraph four times in eight seconds.

And those players started yelling immediately. I mean they were yelling.

This is just conjecture, but I wouldn't be surprised if Mnatsakanov and Konstantinov were not starting to get up from their seats. That would be the natural reaction. I think that's what the majority of people would do if the vehicle is moving and you're yelling. Fetisov was focused on looking ahead, out the window and seeing the pole and the tree, and doesn't remember what they were actually doing.

But we know he was still seated, because he told us so. And the white mark we found on the wall over the bar could have come from his tennis shoe. If it was from his shoe, that could have acted as sort of a brake that kept him from going into the air as quickly as Mnatsakanov and Konstantinov.

It doesn't seem likely that with everything that was going on, with the car drifting across the road and all three players yelling at Gnida, that Fetisov would have left his feet propped up. It seems more likely that, with that kind of urgency, he would have at least taken his feet down from the bar.

In questioning him, though, he did not remember the things that happened immediately before the accident; not even the things that happened to him.

It really seemed to look like a case we could wrap up quickly, despite Gnida's unwillingness to talk.

We sent everything to the state police crime lab, all the blood that had been taken from Gnida, on the night of the accident, and we figured we were going to get a complete analysis from them of everything that was in his system and at that point in time we'd be done and I'd take it up to the prosecutor's office.

They were big on John Gambino, too, because owning the company, he had an obligation to know about Gnida's license being suspended. There's a law against letting people drive who have a suspended license.

And it didn't make it any better for Gambino when another of his drivers was arrested on a traffic warrant in Birmingham on June 16th -- three days after the Wings' accident -- charging him with driving on a suspended license. That certainly made us wonder and when we looked into his background, we wondered more.

He has had some scrapes with the law and we got several phone calls about him, too. Like the ones about Gnida, they were usually things that didn't give us answers, but gave us more questions, more things to look into, more things to wonder about.

Nevertheless, five or six days after the accident we think we're moving along pretty good. Our target date then, for wrapping up the case was June 20 -- exactly seven days after it happened.

But things are getting crazy in some ways. For one, there were endless rumors. Some of them -- with the passage of time -- seem inconsequential and even a little funny. But at the time there was nothing funny about them.

By the Thursday after the accident, I was going nuts. The media was following me around every time I left the office, thinking I was going to slip off and interview somebody. I'd go to put gas in my car and the media would follow me.

So about 2 o'clock on Thursday, I told Patterson I needed to get away and lighten up for a little while and that I'd come back the next day and get at it.

"I'm going to get out of here for a while," I told him. "I've got nothing that needs to be done right now."

He said: "I agree with you; I'm going to do that pretty soon, myself."

There was a bunch of press at the back door when I came out but I told 'em: "Nothing else is going to happen today, whatsoever. You can follow me, if you want to, but I'm going to gas my car, like I did the last time you followed me and after that I'm going to go down and have myself a drink, then I'm going home."

So they all kind of have a laugh at that and I drive away and go to my favorite watering home, the Bowlero Lounge in Royal Oak, and order a cocktail, sit down, and don't even have time to take a sip when my beeper goes off.

It's Patterson. And I'm thinking: "Geez, I just got out of there."

So I call him and ask what's up.

> "While I'm happy to be going home, Vladimir and Sergei still need your thoughts and prayers."
> SLAVA FETISOV

A recovering Slava Fetisov addresses a hospital news conference Wednesday. Red Wings trainer John Wharton is in the background.

Comas may last weeks

Two men responding, but remain critical

BY PATRICIA ANSTETT
Free Press Medical Writer

Detroit Red Wings star Vladimir Konstantinov and team masseur Sergei Mnatsakanov are likely to remain in comas for weeks, though their doctors are reporting signs of subtle improvement.

Both men, particularly Mnatsakanov, are responding to commands, and Konstantinov appeared to wiggle his toes at times when people talked to him in Russian, said Dr. Karol Zakalik, a neurosurgeon and one of two doctors who spoke Wednesday at a media briefing at William Beaumont Hospital in Royal Oak.

When asked what many Detroiters want to know — will Konstantinov play hockey again? — Zakalik declined to answer directly, saying it would be "pure speculation" to comment on Konstantinov's hockey status while he remains in critical condition on a ventilator.

"We'd like Vladimir to return to being a father and a husband, and to awaken," said Zakalik, a key doctor on the team treating the men. "Both men will take a long time" to awaken from their comas; "Konstantinov a longer time" because he has the more severe injury, Zakalik added.

Zakalik defined a long time in a coma as "weeks."

Konstantinov and Mnatsakanov were hospitalized Friday night in critical condition when a limousine carrying them and teammate Slava Fetisov crossed two lanes of traffic on southbound Woodward near Quarton in Birmingham and jumped the curb, smashing into a tree.

They were returning from a golf outing six days after the Red Wings won the Stanley Cup. They were not wearing seat belts.

Limousine driver Richard Gnida, who was wearing a seat belt, may have dozed off at the wheel, Birmingham police say. He was released from the hospital late Sunday with minor injuries — testi-

Please see WINGS, Page 7A

THURSDAY, JUNE 19 -- A subdued Slava Fetisov leaves the hospital. (Detroit Free Prees)

"We just got a report that Konstantinov died," he says.

"You're kidding!"

"No. It's a pretty reliable source. We got it from somebody here in the department who knows a nurse at Beaumont who just called up and said Konstantinov just died."

FRIDAY, JUNE 20 -- A week later the city, slowly, is on its way to recovering from the shock of the accident. (Detroit Free Prees)

Well, the hospital was only about a block and a half away from where I was, so I told him I'd run up there.

I guess I was as white as a ghost, because Diane Krier, the barmaid, asked me what happened.

"I heard Konstantinov just died," I told her, then I jumped in my car and get up there and run through the emergency entrance, down the hall, get on the elevator, up to the floor where they are, the elevator opens up and there is a big Red Wing security guy -- they had people stationed there since the Mnatsakanov incident.

I'm expecting a madhouse, but here's this one security guy kind of standing there going: "Doodly doo do doo," and he says: "How's it going?"

"Oooooookkkk. How's it going with you?"

"OK."

I looked down the hall and I could see Konstantinov's room and there's no people running around or anything like that. So I tell him: " I just heard Konstantinov died."

"No, he didn't die."

"Are you sure? There haven't been any people running in there?"

He goes: "No. Believe me. I would know."

So I said: "OK." and we made some more small talk and there was no activity, so I go back to the bar and tell everybody there that it was just so much BS and I call Patterson and tell him Konstantinov isn't dead.

"OK," he says, "thanks...now go relax like you were going to."

So I sit down, have one sip of my drink and my beeper goes off again.

It's Patterson. Again.

I call him up and say: "What!?"

"Did you see Konstantinov?"

"No, I didn't see him."

"Ah, well, we just got another report. This time, the prosecutors office called and said they have information from a source down there that Konstantinov had died."

"I can't believe that; there was no activity."

"Well, you know, they sometimes hide things like

that."

"Yeah," I go, "but there was no activity...unless, maybe they took him to the operating room or something and that's where it happened."

"Well, everybody's going to start talking about this. You know how rumors spread. Everybody starts calling their favorite news person and we already had that problem."

"OK, I'll go back up there."

So I shoot up there again. Same thing. Run down the hall and all of that kind of stuff, up the elevator and the security guy kind of looks at me and I tell him: "I've got to walk down there to the room."

I go down and peek my head in and there he was sitting there, in a chair, strapped up and it was plain that he was there and he was alive.

So I call Patterson and said: "I've seen him and he's alive, the living, breathing Konstantinov, sitting there."

I go back and sit down and the beeper goes off. Again. And it's Patterson telling me to call the prosecutors office and tell them what I told him. They still were believing their information was good and I kind of had to insist he was alive before they would believe me.

Finally I finished that drink.

And I had one more.

* * *

Another thing that held us up -- something that took a lot more time than that one wild goosechase going back and forth to the hospital to make sure Konstantinov wasn't dead -- was that the phone was ringing off the hook.

I didn't have voice mail until then, but there were so many calls, we had to set it up.

I mean calls from attorneys, everybody involved in Gnida's and Gambino's side of it, probably hundreds of phone calls on every aspect of it. People saying: "This guy's involved in this...this guy does this...this guy does that," and we had to follow up on a lot of it.

We got a phone call from a woman who stated she saw, prior to the time anyone else got there, another party get out of the vehicle. She suggested it was a woman. She was adamant that there was somebody else in the vehicle and that we were covering it up because the woman was in the front seat having sex with the driver when this happened. As you can tell by the pictures and so forth, anyone else in the front seat of that vehicle would have been squashed to smithereens. There could have been no one else inside the vehicle at that time.

Some of the calls like that you just make a quick check and toss out. But a lot of it, you have to look into more seriously.

On June 19th, we got a phone call from an anonymous informant who said a co-worker of hers stated that she knew Gnida had taken a hit of LSD the night before the accident.

I asked if that person would talk to me and the answer was, "no way."

So how do you investigate something like that?

Suspicions aren't proof.

We had calls too from people, anonymous again, saying they were friends of Gnida's and that he was, the words were 'pot head', 'smokes marijuana all the time', 'gets high all the time and falls asleep', you know, those kinds of things.

Exelby secured this search warrant, allowing Gnida's blood to be drawn, because he and two prior offenses for operating a vehicle under the influence, had a suspended license at the time of the accident and had stated he blacked out prior to the accident.

    I could tell from talking to them on the phone that they were probably doing it, too, so none of them wanted to come forward and be identified and get involved.

    None of that is evidence, though.

    None of that proves anything. None of it means anything.

The accident occured at 9:10 p.m. and at 11:03 p.m. two vials of Gnida's blood was taken by a nurse at Beaumont Hospital. What was or was not in that blood would be the center of the entire case.

After enough of those calls, though, I called Felix Adatsi with the Michigan State Police Crime Lab and told him there were rumors that Gnida did acid the night beforehand and No. 2, that we're hearing he's a major marijuana smoker. I told him I didn't know if that made any difference in his tests, but I wanted him to be advised of

```
                    STATE OF MICHIGAN
FSD-96 (11/91)      DEPARTMENT OF STATE POLICE
                      FORENSIC SCIENCE DIVISION
                      EAST LANSING LABORATORY
                         TOXICOLOGY SUBUNIT
                        714 S. HARRISON ROAD
                      EAST LANSING, MI 48823
                        PHONE (517) 336-6191
                         FAX (517) 336-6511

                        TOXICOLOGY REPORT

Laboratory No.: 74882-97                    Record No.        : 5557.97
Received By   : Chitra Gunaga               Date Received     : 06-17-97
Delivered By  : First Class Mail            Time Received     : 09:00 AM
Agency        :                             File Class        : 5400-1
                                            Date Completed    : 06-20-97
                Birmingham Police Dept.     Agency No.        : 97-9513
                P.O. Box 3001, 151 Martin
                Birmingham, MI 48012


Subject : RICHARD GNIDA(A)


Evidence Received:

    1 - Sealed Michigan State Police Specimen Kit (TriTech) containing:
        1 - Tube with approx. 9 ml. blood
        1 - Tube with approx. 9 ml. blood


Results of Analysis:

        Analysis of the blood did not show the presence of opiates,
        amphetamines, barbiturates, benzodiazepines, cocaine
        metabolite or any other acidic, neutral or basic drugs.

        This laboratory does not analyze samples other than urine
        for the presence of cannabinoids (marihuana). The
        sample(s) will be returned upon written request.




                                      Geoffrey A. French
                                      Laboratory Scientist


Public Act 35 of 1994 requires: "The investigating officer of each criminal case being
adjudicated shall advise the prosecuting attorney if a forensic test has been conducted in the case."

           IMPORTANT:  THE SPECIMEN(S) WILL BE DISCARDED 30 DAYS AFTER
                       REPORTED DATE UNLESS INSTRUCTIONS ARE RECEIVED
                       ASKING US TO RETURN SAME.
```

The State Police lab found no evidence of alcohol or drugs in Gnida's blood, but in the letter from Geoffrey French, their laboratory scientist, to our office, it is noted that they don't have the capability to test blood for marijuana.

what we were hearing.

He just kind of said, "Oh, OK."

But before long he called back and said: "I just want to let you know we do not test blood for marijuana or LSD. We don't have the equipment to do that. We could do it with urine, but not with blood."

> **Birmingham Police Department**
> 151 MARTIN STREET
> P.O. BOX 3001
> BIRMINGHAM MICHIGAN 48012
> 313/644-3405
>
> EDWARD P. OSTIN
> Chief of Police
>
> 6/20/97
>
> Narrative Report
>
> Case: #97-9513
>   Personal Injury Accident
>   Woodward and Redding
>   June 13, 1997
>
> At approximately 3:00 p.m. date undersigned received phone call from Mr. Felix Adatsi, technician, Michigan State Police Crime Lab, 714 S. Harrison Rd., East Lansing, Michigan, 48823, phone (517) 336 6191, fax (517) 336-6511. Information received was that the crime lab had finished the testing of the blood sample for one Richard Gnida, DOB 7/31/69, limo driver. Results show no alcohol in blood. Testing was conducted on five (5) main classifications of narcotics. All proved to be negative. Tested were barbiturates, opium, cocaine, amphetamines, and a class of drugs which included valium.
>
> Mr. Adatsi reports that they had received approximately 9 millimeters of blood; they have used approximately one quarter for their testing and to test for LSD and marijuana the samples would have to forwarded to other labs. Mr. Adatsi suggested the use in Lansing of the Toxicology Lab Center, Inc., 5836 Executive Dr., Lansing, Michigan, 48911, technician Mr. James Sedick, phone (517) 882-5791, fax (517) 882-6528. Mr. Adatsi reports that they can test for the presence of marijuana. The Toxicology Lab Centers, Inc. can test for the presence of LSD, but they cannot give a confirmation to the amount of LSD in the blood. That he will research a lab in the state that will be able to test for LSD. At this time, a fax was sent to Michigan State Police Crime Lab, Lansing, Michigan authorizing the release of one (1) blood tube to the Toxicology Lab Centers, Inc. Also a fax was sent to the Toxicology Lab Center, Inc. advising them of our desire for the test of marijuana in the sample.
>
> R. Patterson
> Deputy Chief of Police

Deputy Chief Patterson's narrative report, authorizing the release of blood to the Toxicology Lab Centers in Lansing for marijuana testing.

"You mean it can't be done?" I asked.

"Oh, it can be done in other labs; we just don't have that equipment here,"

If we had gotten a urine sample the night of the accident, we would not have been in this predicament. But Adatsi tried to help and mentioned another lab in Lansing

-- the Toxicology Lab Center -- so I got in touch with them and we asked Adatsi to send them one of the two vials of blood that had been drawn from Gnida at 11:03 Friday night, not quite two hours after the accident.

The next day, Friday the 20th, we received the state police toxicology report stating, "Analysis of the blood did not show the presence of opiates, amphetamines, barbiturates, benzodiazepines, cocaine metabolic or any other acidic, neutral or basic drugs.

"This laboratory does not analyze samples other than urine for the presence of cannabinoids (marijuana). The sample(s) will be returned upon written request."

The 20th was the day we had first hoped to turn the case over to the prosecutor's office, but now -- because of the problem with marijuana and LSD testing -- we were beginning to have to stretch out that timeline.

And it was about to get worse.

On Monday the 23rd, I get notification from the second lab that they can do marijuana testing and pretest for LSD but that is all. They say they can't testify about any LSD presence in court, because they are not expert witnesses in that aspect of it.

Well, we couldn't settle for someone who wasn't going to be an expert on this. What good is that? It's too important, so we've got to find somebody who could testify and we didn't want to wait any longer than necessary.

We'd talked about wrapping up the case on the 20th and the 23rd and now it's the 23rd. I'm not catching any heat from my boss, but I'm catching a lot of pressure from the press, which didn't bother me too bad. But a lot of people are asking, "What's going on? What's going on?" and I'm also taking heat internally from my peers. There were people who thought I was just dragging this thing out. And on top of that there were more and more rumors every day.

So I wanted to get this thing done quick.

We called the FBI lab in Washington, D.C., and they said they could do it, but it would take four to six weeks, because they would have to put it on a schedule behind other cases they already had pending, which I'm sure were just as important. It was very understandable, but we couldn't wait that long.

My wife, Kathy, works in the lab at St. Joseph's Hospital in Pontiac and I called her and asked what they did when they needed something done forensic-wise like that. She put me in touch with Karen Moores, who's in charge of that, and she told me about a lab they use in Pennsylvania: National Medical Services.

She said they are an excellent lab, so I made a call and got hold of Maureen Mitchell, I introduced myself and told her what we were working on and what our problem was.

She said she had heard of it.

"I just want you to know," I said, "we're not going to let your labs name out in regards to this. But if it somehow leaks to the media, you're going to be swamped with newspaper people and all of that stuff."

She was amused that I was making an issue of that.

"We do this sort of thing all the time," she said. "We did O.J. Simpson and we have a procedure on how to handle the press. Don't worry about that."

She told me they could begin testing as soon as they got the blood and that they should have a report in a week or 10 days on the LSD. That was all we were concerned about at that time, because the Lansing lab had marijuana testing in the works and they told us they could testify in regards to its presence in Gnida's blood.

The very next day, the report from the Lansing lab came back completely negative. Negative for LSD and negative for marijuana, which, frankly, surprised me a little bit, with all the rumors we had heard.

Now we've got a driver who won't talk, negative tests for all drugs from the Michigan testings and the results from the National Medical Services won't be back for at least a week, so we shove back the target date for closing the case until July 7.

But we still want to be thorough, to make sure we have looked at everything, so I call Maureen in Pennsylvania and told her: "From what I know about marijuana, I think there should be a trace of it in his system, if he's a smoker. I know it might just be a trace -- not enough to charge him for -- but I'm concerned that the test from Lansing came back zero, complete nothing.

"Shouldn't it have shown something, residue or something like that?"

And she says, "I presume it should come back with something."

"You know what," I told her, "since you've got the blood there, why don't you go ahead and test for marijuana as well as LSD?"

And she says OK.

I told Pernick at the prosecutors office what we were doing and he agreed.

Now we'd have two expert labs looking at it, so we can say it was done thoroughly.

Meanwhile, the media is beginning to say, "Hey, if this

wasn't the Red Wings, we'd be done with this."

But I've had longer cases; once, when I was working in the detective bureau, a guy hit two kids walking across the street and they were left with broken bones, bigtime. That case took over three and a half months. The only difference was, there was no media involved in that one.

So I understood cases sometimes took a long time and so did my administrators.

But the phone calls from the media were constant and one day I got one that turned out to be the first of a series of puzzling and interesting calls.

It was a fellow who identified himself as a reporter for a Russian newspaper.

The first time he called, I just thought he was in a hurry. He said he wanted to know if I could give him some information and I was in the process of telling him what we had when he goes, "OK," and very abruptly hangs up.

The second time, same thing.

He would never leave a message for me to call him back, as most of the media did. I'd get messages from someone in the office that some Russian guy had called me up and every now and then he'd catch me in.

I'd just tell him, like I did the rest of the media, where the investigation had gone and I'd be like in the middle of a sentence and he'd say, "I've got to go," and he'd hang up.

Once he called and said, "We've got to have this done in three minutes."

I told him I'd call him back and he'd tell me that I couldn't because he was switching hotels. I thought it was very apparent that this guy thought he was being followed.

We laughed about it sometimes at the station.

There were conspiracy theories flying around and

all of that, but we weren't putting one bit of credence into it.

And then something happened that made me wonder if we should be laughing about it.

CHAPTER 4

I'd been waiting to talk to John Wharton, the Wings' trainer, because I'd been told he was the guy who could ease the way for me to talk to players I needed to hear from. Carole Ilitch had brought it up that he was at the hospital quite a bit and that it might be best for me to meet him there.

On June 28 we finally connected there.

My first thing was: "How are the players?" because they were not out of the woods by any means, as far as if they were going to make it or not. Technically, if one of these guys dies, you're looking at a much more serious charge.

It was clear from the beginning that John was a very nice gentleman. And I could tell by talking to him that he was deeply concerned, not over them only as players, but as friends.

These were all men who had grown up in a very different place, under a much different system and had moved around the world to become sort of heroes to some people, to the fans. But friends to the people who really knew them.

Konstantinov had grown up in a town north of the Arctic Circle, where the sun shines only two hours a day in the winter and when he joined the Red Army team -- because he looked so much older than his 17 years -- his teammates nicknamed him "Dyadya", grandpa. And while Fetisov insisted on coming here through only the most legal of channels, Konstantinov was permitted to come to the United States only after he pretended to be suffering

The Vladinator, the way we will remember him, playing hard and tough as he crashes into St. Louis Blues goalie Grant Fuhr during a game in April of 1997. (Mary Schroeder/ Detroit Free Press)

from a rare form of cancer, treatable only here.

He was the muscle, the guy they called Vlad the Impaler and the Vladinator; Fetisov was the professional, the politician; Mnatskanov was the healer, the masseur whose hands soothed the players aching muscles.

Wharton is concerned about them on a very personal level and he told me that someone had given him some second hand information that the players were being blackmailed, so to speak. He didn't use that word, but they were being threatened that if anything came out in regards to the accident, that there were some pictures that could be embarrassing to the players.

I wrote a memo that noted:

"Some of the Wings players have been told...that if charges are brought...things will happen. The following quotes were cited:

"'I know where you guys have been all week and what you were doing'."

"'Your wives are going to find out what was happening this week'."

"Wharton is sending word out to all players tonight to reassure them that I'm not investigating them and I will not tolerate extortion impeding my investigation."

This whole thing was getting messy and involved and cluttered by issues that had no bearing on what we were trying to get to, namely: Why did the accident happen? What caused the driver to pass out and lose control of the car?

Nevertheless, all these other things couldn't simply be ignored. I had to consider them and I had to notify the prosecutors office of everything that was going on, so I told them about my conversation with Wharton and was told to keep their office informed regarding the possible

> **CONFIDENTIAL**
>
> June 28, 1997   PI Accident   97-9513
>
> **CONFIDENTIAL INTERVIEW**
>
> During interview with John Wharton at Beaumont Hospital he relayed to me the following facts.
>
> He believes that some of the Wings players have been told by ▇▇▇▇▇▇▇, possibly through hospital sources, that if charges are brought against him that things will happen. The following Quotes were cited:
>
> "I know where you guys have been all week and what you were doing."
>
> "Your wives are going to find out what was happening this week."
>
> Wharton states Dr. David Collon, Team Physician (S10) ▇▇▇-▇▇▇▇, hinted that some pictures are involved. Collon will be contacted Monday 6/30/97.
>
> Wharton is sending word out to all players tonight to reassure them that I am not investigating them and I will not tolerate extortion impeding my investigation.
>
> David Schultz
> Traffic Safety Officer
>
> **CONFIDENTIAL**

One of our "wild goosechases". The Red Wings and the police department got numerous calls alleging one thing or other, about the driver, the players, the owner of the limo company. Most were frivilous, but we had to pursue all but the most ridiculous. This was one of those.

extortion. They requested that I follow up on that vigorously, as anything like that would constitute obstruction of justice.

I also spoke with Dr. David Collon, who is the Red Wings' team physician and also works with the Detroit Lions. He told me the Beaumont hospital public relations

> **Birmingham Police Department**
> 151 MARTIN STREET
> P.O. BOX 3001
> BIRMINGHAM, MICHIGAN 48012
> 313/644-3405
>
> EDWARD P. OSTIN
> Chief of Police
>
> **CONFIDENTIAL**
>
> June 30, 1997   PI Accident   97-9513
>
> Oakland County Prosecutors Office was informed of the Confidential File regarding the possible extortion of Red Wing Players. He requested that this be followed up with vigorously.
>
> This would constitute Obstruction of Justice of our current Investigation and would be our jurisdiction.
>
> I am currently tracking down sources in conjunction with the Red Wing Organization.
>
> Officer David Schultz
> Traffic Safety Officer
>
> **CONFIDENTIAL**

When we informed the Oakland County Prosecutors office of the possible extortion threats, they reacted strongly.

department had contacted him, saying someone had contacted the hospital and stated they shot a roll of film at the golf outing that would be bad for the players if it got out.

Dr. Collon told me he spoke with Steve Yzerman, Darrin McCarty, Mike Vernon and Kris Draper about that and that they all seemed unconcerned.

As far as the accident investigation goes, it doesn't matter what the players did socially that week. But I did not find any shred of evidence that they conducted themselves as anything but gentlemen that entire week. this turned out to be another false rumor.

We're now to July 1 and this thing is grinding on slowly. It seems, instead of tossing off the irrelevant bits of information that are coming in, it is picking up more irrelevant pieces every day.

I've all but forgotten about my conversation dealing with Fetisov's Russian political connection and with the conversations with the Russian writer, when Steve Facione, vice president of Olympia Entertainment, calls to say he wants to talk to me.

Within days of the accident, he says, Mike Ilitch's personal secretary, Colleen, received a phone call from a man with a foreign accent who said, "I tried to warn you in the letter...that accident was not an accident."

I guess they felt about that call like we felt about a lot of ours, that it was just a crank. So they didn't come to us right away.

But around the first of July a similar call was received by a different secretary, Carol. Facione said he didn't know exactly what was said word-for-word, but that the general tone was threatening and that the accident had not been an accident.

I took these conversations with Facione as another sign that the Red Wings' organization wasn't going to hold anything back. They were open with us all the way.

I went to Deputy Chief Patterson with the things I had heard from the Wings, because now we had to explore the possibility -- as remote as it might be -- that

> **City of Birmingham**
> 151 Martin Street
> P.O. Box 3001
> Birmingham, Michigan 48012-3001
> General Offices (810) 644-1800   FAX (810) 644-5614
>
> **July 05, 1997   PI Accident   97-9513**
>
> Spoke with Steve Facione (███████████)
> (███-███-████) Vice President of Olympia Entertainment, owner of the Detroit Red Wings.
>
> Mr. Facione states that within days after the accident, Mike Illitchs' personal secretary Colleen received a phone call from a man with a foreign accent who stated the following "I tried to warn you in the letter. That accident was not an accident". Apparently Collen tried to switch the call to the Security Department and the caller hung up. Mr. Illitch could not recall any such letter.
>
> Within the past few days a similar call was received by a different secretary, Carol. Facione does not know exactly what was said but it was pertaining to it not being an accident and threatening in nature. Carol and Colleen will be on vacation until Monday July 07, 1997, at that time Facione will set up interviews with them.
>
> Officer David Schultz
> Traffic Safety Officer

Some threatening and suspicious telephone calls to the Red Wings office led to this memo and a meeting with FBI Special Agent Charles Whistler, a specialist on the Russian Mafia.

somehow this accident had something to do with the fact the players in the limo were Russians and that Fetisov was seen by some as a political figure, or a potential political figure, in Russia after he finished playing hockey.

I tried to make contact with the FBI about the situation, but I got nowhere, so I went back to Patterson and told him I had called them and nothing came of it. He called and the next day a special agent came out.

His name was Charles Whistler and he is the Detroit area's expert on Russia. He's been there, met with KGB in a joint-type session on the Russian Mafia, how it works, how it operates and so forth. So I knew I was dealing with someone who knew the territory.

He knew a lot more about Fetisov's political status than I did.

The New Jersey Devils had tried to get him to defect from the Soviet Union in the early '80s, but Fetisov, being a man of some character and integrity, told them he was not interested in coming to the United States that way.

His long years of playing hockey in the USSR had established him as a person of loyalty and patriotism. He was, to young hockey players there, the epitome of what it meant to play the sport.

So he stayed and won the legal right to play in the NHL, which established a new personal and economic freedom not just for himself, but for all the Soviet and Russian athletes who would follow. That is what established him as a power over there far beyond what he could accomplish merely as a hockey player.

Whistler laid down a lot of facts. He talked about how the president of the Russian Ice Hockey federation is actually a political job, not like being the commissioner of the NHL. It is part of the government, so to speak. He also brought up that over the years, a lot of money was made through the Red Army team. That's how they brought in like blue jeans and video tapes, from western countries, smuggling in goods that they weren't supposed to have, to

Russian Hockey Chief Slain

■ MOSCOW—The president of Russia's Ice Hockey Federation was shot and killed outside his country house in what police said was an apparent contract killing.

Unidentified gunmen opened fire on Valentin Sych as he and his wife approached their car outside their home near the village of Ivantsevo, north of Moscow, a federation spokesman said. Sych's wife, Valentina, was seriously wounded and taken to a hospital.

Sych, 59, won the federation's top post in 1994 in a bitter power struggle with former hockey chief Vladimir Petrov. The following year, a Moscow court reinstated Petrov to the post, but Sych refused to step down. The two men eventually settled the feud privately, with Sych retaining his post.

The hockey federation was one of several sports organizations formerly permitted by tax laws to import alcohol and tobacco duty-free, usually reselling them commercially for large profits. The newspaper Izvestia said Sych was heavily involved in such transactions before the loophole was closed this year.

—Associated Press

Whistler emphasized the power of the Russian Mafia and the political implications of the Russian hockey presidency and faxed me copies of stories about the assasination of Valentin Sych two months before the limo crash. Because Fetisov's stature in Russia and his potential political plans in the future, we had to wonder if the Mafia had a hand in teh accident. (Washington Post - 4-23-97)

resell. The government, basically, knew it was going on but they closed their eyes to it. They didn't look at it as being really big-time illegal.

They could have shut it down in a heartbeat.

But things have changed there now and the Russian Mafia really wants a part of that and the government is very against it. Speculation was, for a long time, that when Fetisov was done playing hockey that that is how he would start, Whistler said.

That he would take over the hockey federation.

I'm going, 'OK, where are we going here?'

And that's where he brings up Valentin Sych. Sych had been the president of the Russian Ice Hockey Federation and two months before the limo crash, he was shot to death outside Moscow in what was described as a contract killing. His wife was seriously wounded at the same time.

Machine-gunned.

No one had ever mentioned that to me before. I just go, like 'Wow!'

He told me that speculation was, obviously, it was

done by the Russian Mafia.

The other thing he had brought up was that they had been trying to make contact with the Russian players for a couple of years because the FBI had heard they were being extorted, all throughout the NHL.

At the end, he said he would assist us in any way they could and my only thoughts were, A number one, give us the name of any kind of drugs they know the Russian Mafia is using that we could test for; and the other thing would be to contact their people to put their ears to the ground, so to speak, just to see if they could pick anything up. We're not putting a lot of credence in this, but it's got to be checked out and if there's anything to it, there's got to be some word out there somewhere.

When he got back to his office, he faxed me copies of stories about Sych's murder.

Later, we contacted Maureen at NMS again, and asked her to run tests for the drugs that the Russians were known to use, things that could be slipped into drinks, anything like that.

At the same time that all of this is going on, I'm trying to get a better grasp on just who Richard Gnida is. Frankly, before I began talking to them, I didn't expect I'd care much for the other drivers, especially after the accident, followed just a few days later by another of Gambino's drivers being stopped and arrested in Birmingham.

I figured all of these guys were pretty much the same, after that.

But I was wrong.

They were helpful, they were straight up and they were a good and helpful group of people.

One of them was a fellow named Frank Cooper, who

does maintenance work for one of the car rental companies at Metro Airport and drives part-time because his wife is ill and the family needs the extra money for medical expenses.

He drove Nicklas Lidstrom and Tomas Sandstrom on the night of the accident.

He knew Gnida slightly, because they had worked a wedding together once before. Beyond that, he didn't know much about him.

They made some smalltalk at the course and Cooper said Gnida seemed "excited" about being around the Red Wing players. He was so excited, in fact, that at one point he left the area where the limos were parked and went out on the golf course.

Cooper comes across as very professional. The guys are supposed to stay by their cars; they can crawl in and take a snooze if they're going to be there for another couple of hours, but they know they can't leave their cars.

So, understanding that Gnida going out on the course wasn't typical, or acceptable, behavior from a driver, Cooper called Gambino's office at approximately 4:30 and told them about him being on the course.

Cooper said that pretty soon someone from Gambino's paged them and told the drivers to get off of the course. Cooper said he thought there was one other driver out there with Gnida, but did not know which one it was.

He said that the times he saw Gnida at the course, he didn't appear drunk, high or tired.

Keith Berra was another of the drivers. He had worked for Gambino for about 3 1/2 years and had known Gnida most of that time. But on the day of the accident, he drove some of the players wives around and wasn't at the golf course.

In general, the other drivers really didn't know much about Gnida. They said he didn't hang around with them, that he was sort of a loner and people hadn't seen him with any girls. Usually, when he drove for Gambino, he drove by himself, not with a group of drivers. And usually he got the dirt jobs, the crummy jobs that nobody else wanted to do.

He just hung around Gambino's place.

Now the prosecutor's office is big on Gambino in this case, too, and so are some people in the Wings' organization. The Wings are angry with him, because they figure he should know about his driver having a suspended license and we've had those calls about Gambino-this and Gambino-that...and then we had the fact that his attorney had contacted us early on and told us that absolutely, no way, would Gambino cooperate on anything.

On June 28th we had requested a search warrant of Gambino's offices in Belleville in order to get Gnida's employment records, to determine if they showed his driving suspension. But when we made our search there was no file there on Gnida at all, nothing. Zip. Zero.

That was the only time I saw Gambino. He was at the top of the stairs when we got there and he walked into a door. I just saw him for seconds.

But, of course, we're getting all sorts of phone calls on him, at least partially, I suspect, because of his name.

There are people making connections with the New York Gambinos and saying he's involved in shady things and that anyone who works for him must be shady and so forth.

There's always conspiracy theories out there. Look at Kennedy or at Princess Di. Because this accident is what it is -- and without ever being able to get into Gnida's head -- it was natural that there would be theories like that connected with it. You can lend credence to every one of them but at some point you go on. You say, "We've checked this as much as we can."

That's the way it was with Gambino, because some people were raising the question of a New York involvement in this accident now.

It was another one of those things we had to look into. No matter how far fetched.

You get to know people in this business after a while and I made contact with someone who had a connection where they could make an inquiry of the family in New York. And basically they brought back that no one knew him.

This person made a number of inquiries, here and in New York, and the people in New York knew the name -- maybe because of the wreck -- but there was no connection.

We came up with absolutely nothing that led us to believe there was any involvement by the New York Mafia, nor that Gambino was anything other than the owner of a limo company. And about the same time we came to that conclusion -- around the middle of July -- Facione and Tim Sopha, the chief security officer for the Olympia Corporation came back to us about the phone calls that had caused us to look at conspiracy and get the FBI involved in the first place.

They had gone to Mike Ilitch with everything and after checking they found that there had never been any

> **City of Birmingham**
>
> 151 Martin Street
> P.O. Box 3001
> Birmingham, Michigan 48012-3001
>
> General Offices (810) 644-1800   FAX (810) 644-5614
>
> **July 17, 1997   PI Accident   97-9513**
>
> **Informational Meeting**
>
> **Present**
>
> **Steve Facione (Fah choe knee)**
> **Group Vice President**
> **Olympia Corporation**
>
> **Tim Sopha**
> **Chief Security Officer**
> **Olympia Corporation**
>
> **Informed Sopha and Facione of the status of our investigation. Informed them of what to expect in the future in the investigation and that we will keep them informed as possible.**
>
> **Facione informed me that there has been no more calls at all implying a threat to the Russian players. He informed that there never was a threat or letter previous to the accident. He apologized for the mix-up and assured me there was nothing else to it.**
>
> **David Schultz**
> **Traffic Safety Officer**

After spending time chasing down the Russian Mafia angle, Red Wings vice president Steve Facione and security officer Tim Sopha tell me the whole thing seemed to be a mistake from the beginning.

letter warning that anything bad was going to happen. They said they hadn't received any more phone calls of that type, either, and that they didn't think there was any cause to put any credence in the earlier ones.

The deal was they really didn't want a lot of hoopla and all of that stuff and they wanted it all done kind of

Konstantinov stirs from coma

But doctors warn there's no guarantee improvement will continue

BY PATRICIA ANSTETT
Free Press Medical Writer

Red Wings defenseman Vladimir Konstantinov is showing more signs of emerging from a coma, opening his eyes and giving more-consistent physical responses to his family, teammates and doctors.

Konstantinov also is gradually being weaned from a ventilator for short periods, and a device that monitored the threat of increased pressures on the brain was removed Tuesday.

But doctors at William Beaumont Hospital in Royal Oak, where Konstantinov has been since the June 13 limousine crash that also left team masseur Sergei Mnatsakanov in a coma, counseled against excessive optimisim Tuesday, saying that patients emerging from comas, as Konstantinov appears to be doing, have day-to-day fluctuations.

"It's a long road ahead," said spokeswoman Colette Stimmell, reporting the physicians' assessment.

Weaning Konstantinov from the ventilator could take several more days, if not weeks, she added.

A statement Beaumont released to the news media Tuesday afternoon said Konstantinov "continues to make purposeful movements in response to family, teammates and medical staff, opening his eyes and squeezing his hands on command."

Purposeful, rather than involuntary movement, is a key measurement of recovery in comatose patients.

As good as Tuesday's signs were, doctors look for even more consistency in response to commands, and patients need to have their eyes open more often to be considered conscious and out of a coma.

Teammates were buoyed by the news.

"Obviously, he's not out of the

Please see RECOVERY, Page 2A

Sergei Mnatsakanov  Vladimir Konstantinov

WEDNESDAY, JUNE 25 -- The best news yet. (Detroit Free Press)

quietly and I understood that. Once they told me there was no letter and no more phone calls, it came off as another hoax.

Whistler reported back about that time, too, that his people were hearing nothing to tie the limo accident to anything concerning the Russian Mafia and our tests for the possible drugs had come back negative, so we pretty much put that one to rest.

There was one more, real long sort of conspiracy idea, though.

We got at least one phone call telling us that Gnida was sick and depressed and that there was a chance that his illness caused him to think about taking his own life.

Maybe it was just that simple.

Maybe he just aimed at the tree and wham! hit it on purpose.

I contacted his attorney, James O'Connell, and told him what we had heard and asked if he would talk to Gnida about his health. He did and he got back to us with the information that there was nothing like that which could be substantiated.

So with that we pretty much put the conspiracy theories behind us and got back to what we were trying to determine all along: Why did that car run into the tree?

CHAPTER 5

We had sent Gnida's blood away to National Medical Services in Philadelphia on June 23 to check for LSD and then had sort of complicated their job by asking them to check for marijuana, too. And, they were also checking for drugs that could have been slipped to Gnida.

So we had given them a load.

But they were, really, about the end of the line for us.

We had been looking at this for more than three weeks and, despite all the accusations and innuendoes, all the leads and tips and the wild goose chases, we really were no closer to determining what made Richard Gnida leave the roadway that night and hit that tree.

We knew he hadn't -- as that one caller claimed -- had a woman in the front seat with him.

We knew Konstantinov, Fetisov, and Mnatsakanov had screamed at him from the time the limousine first started moving to the left. And we knew he did nothing to correct the move. He didn't cut the steering wheel back, he didn't apply the brakes, he didn't do anything.

Maybe he had been passed out, for whatever reason.

But then we thought of something else. What if he had been on the cars cell phone? What if he had been distracted, as so many people are, by talking on the phone and simply lost control of the car because of that?

It was not a question Fetisov could answer. And it wasn't a question that either Gnida or Gambino -- who had refused to cooperate -- would answer.

So we decided to check the car over again, see about

the cell phone, see if we could get its number and check the records to find out if Gnida was on the phone at the time of the accident -- a little after 9 o'clock on the night of June 13.

Now this car, by now, has been torn apart a bunch of times. We did it on the Monday after the accident, when Larry Richardson and I, and the state drug dog, went over the car.

And, because it was evident from the moment of the accident that there would be law suits filed as a result, the insurance company USF&G --Gambino's insurer -- looked at the car. And Konstantinov's attorney, Jim Bellanca, had people examine it, too. The Ford Motor Company people would eventually go over it and Konstantinov would have a second group look at it.

When I say *look at it*, I don't mean *look at it*; I mean examine it closely. From top to bottom, inside and outside. Everything. Everybody was looking for a cause, for a place to put fault. For something to blame.

So that limo had been gone over pretty good.

But nobody had any reason to do any kind of check on the car phone.

A friend of mine is an electronics guy, Harold Paulsen. I asked him to come by and see if he could help me determine if there had been a phone and how we could find its records.

There are different carriers out there, Ameritech and this and that. You've got to know what you're looking for and we weren't getting any cooperation from the limousine company. We asked Gambino's attorney, Daniel Blank, and he said they weren't giving us anything.

But Paulsen told me there's a way to pick up the

Birmingham Police Department
151 MARTIN STREET
P.O. BOX 3001
BIRMINGHAM, MICHIGAN 48012
313/644-3405

EDWARD P. OSTIN
Chief of Police

July 09, 1997   P1 Accident 97-9513

Contacted Harold Paulsen of Sound Installations in Royal Oak. Paulsen agreed to go over to limosine with this officer in an attempt to locate cellular phone number of the limosine. We were unable to locate the handset at this time.

While in back of limosine Paulsen pointed an object laying on ground just to the rear of the drivers seat. The object appeared to be a marijuana cigarette and was retrieved and will be sent to the lab for analysis. See follow up on this matter.

David Schultz
Traffic Safety Officer

What began as a search for a cell phone, turned into something else -- the discovery of what appeared to be an old marijuana butt in the limo, almost a month after the accident. I discounted its importance from the beginning, but not everyone did.

phone and dial something in and it'll tell you what company it is, then you can go from there and search the company's records.

So we needed to find the telephone.

Well, we go in and get in the front seat area and it's just like crushed, compacted. You can see where there's a mounting for a phone, but we can't find an instrument. Everything's all ajar, so we crawl into the back of the limo and we're poking around between the passenger's compartment, looking with flashlights into every little crack and space to see if we can see a headset and that's when my buddy goes: "Hey! Look at that!"

And I go: "Oh, shit!"

"Is that what I think it is?"

"It sure looks like it is," I said.

And I reached down and picked it up and here's this marijuana cigarette butt. Now we've got something else to look at.

From the minute I found it, I put no credence in it having anything to do with the accident. And I was surprised at how much was made of it as the case went on.

But you've got to do what you've got to do, and with that thing in my hand, I knew we had to submit it to National Medical Services and give them one more thing to screen.

I don't think that joint was there the night of the accident. But it was all dried up and old looking, so who knows how long it had been there?

I'm not naive enough to believe people don't smoke marijuana in a limousine. I imagine that's a place where a lot of it happens. But because of that, I figure there's about 2,000 suspects who might have smoked that joint.

A lot of things could have caused that thing to be there when we found it.

Possibly it had been in that car for a long time and was under the car's carpeting or a floor mat or wedged in somewhere, stuck. Maybe that's why the drug dog didn't show much interest when it sniffed around the car. Then it

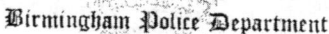

The letter that -- in my mind -- turned the case. Deputy Chief Patterson authorized the forwarding of Gnida's blood to the National Medical Services lab in Pennsylvania.

got jarred loose, knocked around by all of the people pulling the car apart and putting it back together again. The seats had been taken out and moved around by myself and Richardson, by Bellenca's people and by those other groups.

I'm certainly not suggesting in any way that somebody planted it there.

What happened was, either it had been there long before the accident and just hadn't shown up until Paulsen and I found it on July 9, or -- and maybe this is a stretch -- perhaps somebody got his girlfriend in there after the accident and said: "Hey, this is where the Red Wings' accident happened," and they smoked a joint.

We don't make a public issue of finding the joint right away, but the next day -- July 10 -- out of the blue, Gnida's attorney, James O'Connell, calls me and says that Gnida wants to talk to me. He says that he could provide evidence that Gambino knew Gnida's license was suspended.

Now, to me, the fact that he wanted to talk indicated he believed he was going to be charged with something more serious than just a suspended license. When you look at it, if Gnida and O'Connell thought he was just going to be charged with a suspended license, they wouldn't have offered anything. I'm sure they thought it was going to be a much higher charge.

It had seemed to us all along that Gambino knew about Gnida's driving record. Everything points to it, but there was nothing concrete to prove it beyond a doubt.

Through the news media, we had heard that Gambino's secretary was supposed to do the checking on driver's records, but he never told us anything, himself.

Public opinion and the press at the time, seemed to have turned their anger from Gnida to Gambino. Most people seemed to believe Gambino must have known about Gnida's record, or should have known about it. And at the same time, we heard that it was Gambino that the Red Wings' organization was really angry with.

We were now almost a month past the night of the

accident and Fetisov, who suffered relatively minor chest and lung injuries in the crash, had long been out of the hospital. As a matter of fact on July 9, the day Paulsen and I found the joint in the limo, Fetisov had been in Sinai Hospital in New York, where his daughter was born with heart problems in 1991. But while he was out and about, Mnatsakanov and Konstantinov were still in serious condition back at Beaumont Hospital.

So O'Connell tells me: "Maybe we can work out a deal before my guy is charged."

I asked what he was talking about and he said something like, Gnida could give us information, both verbally and written, that would establish beyond a reasonable doubt that Gambino knew he was a suspended driver.

Well, every bit of information helps, but the point is when you're negotiating things like that, you don't negotiate on the charge. At least, you don't do it in Oakland County. What you offer is that the prosecutor and the police might make recommendations that would weight on any sentence. But he wanted to make a deal regarding what charges were going to be going in...and we would not do that.

I phoned Halushka, one of the assistant prosecutors, and told him about the call and he concured 100 percent. A number one, if you want anything from us, be forthcoming and tell us what happened and tell us anything you know about Gambino and testify and take a polygraph test. If he did that, we could go to bat for him when he was being sentenced, by letting the judge know he had cooperated on both the accident and the owner of the limousine company.

When I told O'Connell that, he seemed frustrated.

> **Birmingham Police Department**
> 151 MARTIN STREET
> P.O. BOX 3001
> BIRMINGHAM, MICHIGAN 48012
> 313/644-3405
>
> EDWARD P. OSTIN
> *Chief of Police*
>
> July 28, 1997   PI Accident 97-9513
>
> Spoke with James O'Connell, Richard Gnidas attorney who states that his client no longer wants to talk with this department. I expressed my concern that he advised he was coming in on Saturday and that he didn't show or call. Originally he said he was coming in to be interviewed and then refused to answer any questions. Twice since that time he has refused to show when he said he would.
>
> With this background in mind I indicated to O'Connell my concern for him surrendering Richard Gnida in a timely fashion, if and when an arrest warrant is issued. O'Connell stated he was a busy man and cannot always return phone calls. I informed him that I wanted a telephone number and current address on Gnida within 24 hours or I would advise my superiors of such and appropriate action would be taken.
>
> This officer has lost confidence in O'Connell as being forthright in this investigation and as such wants verification that Richard Gnida is readily available to answer to any charges. I would also like to personally ask Mr. Gnida his position as to any questioning.
>
> David Schultz
> Traffic Safety Officer

Throughout the case I had doubts about and problems with, Gnida's attorney, James O'Connell. By this time, I was done with him.

I could tell he didn't like my answer. But I told him to take it to Gnida, discuss it and let Gnida make the decision on what he wanted to do.

That was on Thursday, July 10th and I guess it is the next day or two, I see Dave Gorcyca, the Oakland County Prosecutor, on television, saying that probably Gnida will be charged with only driving on a suspended license, if the drug tests come back negative.

Within 24 hours I get a phone call from Mr. Halushka to bring my case up to them. They wanted to review it. It's the morning of Monday, July 14.

Well, everything we've got so far is negative, negative, negative. That's what the State Police lab said, that's what the lab in Lansing said and that's what National Medical Services said about LSD. But we haven't heard from them on marijuana.

I figure I'm going to go up there to the prosecutors office and argue my case. When I heard that on television about possibly just charging Gnida with a suspended license, it was the first time I had heard the prosecutors office talking like that. From the beginning, they had talked about something more substantial, something that actually related to why the accident happened. They had given me every indication that the bare minimum they were going to go after was felonious driving, which I believe would be the right charge.

So I'm planning to go up there, present my case and tell them the way I think it should be, though in the end it is the prosecutor's decision. But you're looking at serious injury.

I wanted to make sure all of the paper work was in order and that everything was right for them. That all the loose ends were tied up. I wanted to have everything that they were going to ask for. But the one thing I did not have, was the results of the marijuana testing that I sent to NMS.

So after I get off the phone with Halushka, I phone

National Medical Services and I get Maureen Mitchell on the phone.

I tell her: "I've got all these tests back, except the one for marijuana and I'm going to need your report on that."

"Hold on just a second," she says. "I think I saw some paperwork on that this morning and I can fax you a copy. Let me see if I can find it."

So she's gone from the phone for just a little while and when she comes back, she says, very nonchalantly, "OK, uh, positive for marijuana."

"What!?!"

"Positive for marijuana."

"Oh, OK. Well, what are you talking about? This guy smoked a joint at a concert a week before, or what?"

"No," she said. "He smoked a joint approximately three to six hours before the blood was taken."

I was just, like, flabbergasted.

She read the numbers to me and read the report.

"So, this guy was under the influence?"

"Well," she said, "we don't say that. We just say that it was in his system and can say he smoked a joint in that point in time."

As soon as I get off the phone to her, I called the prosecutors office, because they were expecting me out there in a few hours with all my paperwork. And they had scheduled a press conference for the next day, too. I got Halushka on the phone.

"Jim, remember I sent a second test to Pennsylvania?"

"Yeah."

"Well, it came back positive."

> **Birmingham Police Department**
> 151 MARTIN STREET
> P.O. BOX 3001
> BIRMINGHAM, MICHIGAN 48012
> 313/644-3405
>
> EDWARD P. OSTIN
> Chief of Police
>
> **July 14, 1997   PI Accident   97-9513**
>
> Contacted James Halushka of the Oakland County Prosecutors Office. After a brief update of status of case it was determined that I would present it to there office on Tuesday July 15, 1997. Mr. Halushka asked if I could informally drop it off sometime in the afternoon on the 14th. I replied I would.
>
> At approximately 11 AM on this date I contacted Maureen Mitchell of National Medical Services for an update on the marijuana test I had there lab run. I was informed it was positive. I asked her to give me the numbers in terms easy to understand.
>
> Three different tests were run on the marijuana. According to Ms. Mitchell it indicates he smoked marijuana within a few hours of the accident. She further stated a Toxicologist would have to evaluate what the levels indicate in regards to Gnidas ability to drive.
>
> This information was forwarded to the Prosecutors office. The Warrant drop off was canceled and a joint press conference was called.
>
> David Schultz
> Traffic Safety Officer

Just when the Oakland County prosecutors office wants to wrap up the case neatly with a press conference, the bombshell hits when Maureen Mitchell at National Medical Services tells me her test on Gnida's blood indicates he smoked marijuana within hours before the accident.

"What!?"

I told him exactly what Maureen told me. It wasn't that he smoked a joint at a rock concert a month beforehand; it was that he had smoked the day of the accident. And I could tell, even over the phone, that he wasn't happy with the news.

I wasn't trying to jam anybody up, but I was excited, because finally we had a reason for the accident that made sense. I guess I expected the prosecutor's office to be excited about it, too.

When Gorcyca announced the toxicology showed there had been marijuana in Gnida's system, all hell broke loose.

Though Halushka hadn't seemed pleased when he heard the news from me the day before, Gorcyca sounded pleased when he talked to the press.

He said: "Something didn't make sense," about Gnida's driving and indicated the presence of marijuana made things more clear. "It didn't make any sense why he should veer from one lane all the way over without braking."

Gorcyca did say that it could take weeks to determine how recently Gnida had used the drug, but I had already been told by the people at National Medical Services that, based on the level of toxins in his system, he had smoked three to six hours before the blood was taken.

Not three to six hours before the accident, but three to six hours before the blood was taken -- which was two hours after the accident. If they were right, that meant he smoked sometime between 5 and 8 p.m. and the accident happened at 9:13 p.m.

Oakland County's Chief Medical Examiner, L.J. Dragovic, told the press that it was possible to determine, sometimes within a matter of hours, when a person injested drugs, by measuring the active ingredients in the blood. That's what NMS did for us. But Dragovic said it was difficult to determine what impact marijuana has on each individual user.

Marijuana is different from alcohol in the way we

National Medical Services, Inc.
Toxicology Specialists Worldwide Since 1970

3701 Welsh Road
Willow Grove, PA 19090
Phone: (215) 657-4900
1-800-522-6671
Fax: (215) 657-2972

uly 14, 1997

TO: Birmingham Police Department
Richard Patterson
151 Martin Street
Birmingham, MI 48012

PRELIMINARY TOXICOLOGY REPORT OF: GNIDA, Richard (Case No. 97-9513)
NMS Control No. 929774
NMS Accession No. 97-109176

EXAMINATION: Analysis Requested - Test No. 0960 - Cannabinoids; Test No. 1866 - Drug Screen II

SPECIMENS: One (1) labelled grey top tube containing — 7 mL blood was received.

FINDINGS:

Blood

DELTA-9 THC   1.0 nanog/mL
(by GC/MS)

11-HYDROXY-THC   None Detected
(by GC/MS)   Reporting Limit: 5.0 nanog/mL

9-CARBOXY-THC   16 nanog/mL
(by GC/MS)

NOTE: Test No. 1866 - Drug Screen II -- PENDING

COMMENTS:

Marihuana is a DEA Schedule I hallucinogen. Pharmacologically, it has depressant and reality distorting effects.

Delta-9-THC is the principle psychoactive ingredient of marihuana/hashish. It rapidly leaves the blood, even during smoking, falling to below detectable levels within several hours. Its active metabolite, 11-Hydroxy-THC, may also fall below detectable levels shortly after inhalation. Delta-9 carboxy THC is the non-active metabolite of Delta-9-THC which peaks 20 to 30 min. after smoking and may be detected for up to one day or more.

Reported peak plasma levels of Delta-9-THC following the smoking of a cigarette containing 10 mg of Delta-9-THC were achieved within 10 min. and ranged from 10 to 26 nanog/mL (0.01 to 0.03 mcg/mL); by 2 hr., the levels declined to less than 5 nanog/mL (0.005 mcg/mL).

Respectfully,

Michael D. Robertson, Ph.D.
Forensic Toxicologist

MDR:seh

****   ****   ANALYSIS SUMMARY   ****   ****

Test No. 0960 - Cannabinoids - Gas Chromatography/Mass Spectrometry on Blood for:
DELTA-9-THC, 11-HYDROXY-THC and 9-CARBOXY-THC.

Test No. 1866 - Drug Screen Panel II - Gas Chromatography of Extracts on Blood for:
PENDING.

****   ****   END OF REPORT   ****   ****

NMS's letter details -- in medical terms -- what they found in Gnida's blood.

Limo driver's test shows marijuana

BY BRIAN MURPHY
Free Press Staff Writer

Limousine driver Richard Gnida had traces of marijuana in his blood the night he crashed into a tree injuring two Detroit Red Wings players and a team masseur, a new reading of blood samples revealed Monday.

But authorities said the samples will have to be analyzed again by toxicologists to determine when Gnida ingested the drug and what role, if any, it may have had in causing his stretch limousine to drift across three lanes of Woodward and slam head-on into a tree.

The accident happened June 13. The blood samples were drawn the same night at the hospital.

Traces of marijuana can stay in the bloodstream for up to a month, and it could take weeks to determine how recently Gnida had used the drug before the crash, Oakland County Prosecutor David Gorcyca told reporters at a news conference Monday.

Gorcyca said DNA tests also will be conducted on a partly smoked marijuana cigarette police found under the driver's seat to determine whether it holds saliva matching Gnida's.

"What a witch-hunt!" reacted Gnida's lawyer, James O'Connell, who called suggestions Gnida was smoking marijuana or was high while at the wheel

Please see GNIDA, Page 2A

TUESDAY, JULY 15 -- At last! The link that would explain why Gnida ran into that tree. It would solve everything. That's what I thought, anyway.

calculate the amount that is in someones system. There is a legal limit at which we say someone is impaired, is drunk, incapable of driving or functioning properly, after drinking. We don't have a limit, don't have numbers like that for marijuana, because while alcohol is legal within limits, marijuana is illegal. Period.

So we don't have defined numbers that say when a person is impaired because of marijuana.

The report from NMS spelled out some very specific numbers, relating how much Delta-9-THC and how much 9-Carboxy-THC were in Gnida's system. The numbers (1.0 nanog/mL in the first test and 16 nanog/mL in the second) mean nothing to the layman, but NMS found both substances in the blood and their report plainly spelled out their belief that he had smoked shortly before the accident.

It stated:"Delta-9-THC is the principle psychoactive ingredient of marihuana/hashish. It rapidly leaves the blood, even during smoking, falling below detectable levels in several hours...Delta-9 carboxy THC is the non-active metabolite of Delta-9-THC which peaks 20 to 50 min. after smoking and may be detected for up to one day or more."

Since Delta-9-THC disappears from the system within several hours -- yet they found traces of it in Gnida's blood -- the implication was that he had smoked shortly before the accident.

Of course, O'Connell, went ballistic at the news.

"What a witch-hunt," he said to the newspapers. He called the report from NMS "a total stretch."

"Do you think they are treating him like someone who didn't have a couple of Red Wings in the back seat? Anyone else in this situation, would pay their fines and be sent home."

But we would have done the same thing in any kind of injury accident of this magnitude. The fact that it was a high profile case had nothing to do with it. In fact, maybe the fact that it was high profile, eventually worked in Gnida's favor, instead of against him, because some of the media and some of the public bought into O'Connell's argument.

It seemed we were going back-and-forth, saying one time that the drug tests had been negative, then coming back and saying they were positive. And there was a faction that certainly seemed to believe we were going to whatever lengths we could to get this guy.

Certainly that wasn't the case.

Some of the drug tests, such as the one at the hospital the night of the accident, was just a cursory, intended to find if the patient needed to be detoxed immediately. Others were complicated by us not taking urine.

We weren't going out of our way to *get* this guy.

But my point was that there had to be a reason for him losing control of the car, hitting that tree and seriously injuring innocent people.

With the report from the National Medical Services, I believed I finally had the reason.

CHAPTER 6

We had, it seemed, the one piece of evidence we had been searching for since the night the limo hit the tree on Woodward and the lives of a bunch of people were changed forever.

But the problem, I think, for the prosecutor's office was that they had already announced the drug tests had come back negative; now they were saying they had a positive one. They had prepared everyone for the lesser charge and they had even scheduled the press conference to announce that and now they couldn't say that.

There were people, some in the press and some of the public that just thought now that we were just looking for anything to stick it to this guy.

The prosecutors office wasn't getting very good positive vibes from the media about charging this guy. I even heard some cameramen at press conferences question what was going on, like this guy was being persecuted.

It's funny, because the Red Wings were involved, celebrities, guys who were heroes to a lot of people, who could get a million people to come downtown for a parade after they won the Stanley Cup, you figured the most likely scenario would be that the guy who was responsible for those serious injuries stood more of a chance of being over-charged than under-charged. But that's not the way it worked.

I'm convinced the prosecutors office was basically almost doing a private public opinion poll. I think they wanted to do what made the prosecutors office look best. They'd had a series of problems. Of course, there's always Dr. Jack Kevorkian and there was a case were a guy shot his dog and at first they weren't going to charge him, and when the media criticized that, they came back and charged him.

I think they just didn't want to take any chances with this.

Their thing was that they needed someone to testify that Gnida was under the influence of narcotics when the accident happened, but there's no acceptable level of illegal narcotics in a person's system as there is with alcohol, so that presented a problem.

There were a lot of things being said that seemed to conflict. Our report from National Medical Services said their tests proved Gnida smoked marijuana as recently as six hours before his blood was taken, and possibly as recently as three hours. Dragovic, Oakland County's medical examiner, concurred -- in an interview with the Detroit Free Press -- that it is possible to determine, sometimes within a matter of hours, when a person took drugs. But when Gorcyca made some statements that marijuana could remain in your system up to 30 days, I began to believe something was amiss.

I had thought, once we got the report from NMS, that we would move ahead pretty quickly, but it was just the opposite.

Another thing that confused matters, too, was that marijuana butt Harold Paulsen and I found in the limo. It was another factor, I think, in the people believing there was a lot of stretching going on to try to pin something on Gnida. I put no credibility in the joint from the beginning, but the public at this point in time was turning around it's opinion of what was going on. It was almost like what happened with the Monica Lewinsky deal. It started out:

"Get the President!" but changed to "Get Ken Starr!"

A very similar thing, I think, happened in this case.

So, instead of the case picking up steam, there was a lull.

The most productive idea at the time was that Phil Pridmore, Oakland County's toxicologist suggested we could use this as a test case to establish guide lines with drugs as we do with alcohol, where .10 blood alcohol is over the legal limit to drive in most states. If we could establish a number that says: Over this point with marijuana, you are under the influence, it would be helpful. His idea was: What better case to establish it on, here is a county with a lot of money and a high-profile case like this.

We could bring in 10 of the top toxicologists in the country and have a discussion and possibly set a limit and propose the legislature make it a law.

The National Medical Services released all our information to him, at our request, but Pridmore couldn't just insert himself into the case and the prosecutors office never moved on it because they were trying another tactic. They were looking for someone who could testify to what marijuana does to behavior.

I wasn't hearing anything from them and "what's going on?" was basically my question.

They wanted someone to say this guy was stoned and nobody does that.

They contacted a person in Maryland, who had researched people's behavior in this type of thing. She isn't a toxicologist, she is like a behavioral scientist type person, who sits there and lets everybody smoke joints, then studies their behavior. They don't tell me who she is right away but they tell me it's a female and that she's top-notch.

```
                    Birmingham Police Department
                         151 MARTIN STREET
                           P.O. BOX 3001
                      BIRMINGHAM, MICHIGAN 48012
                           313/644-3405

EDWARD P. OSTIN
   Chief of Police


       July 28, 1997       PI Accident 97-9513

       Spoke with Jim Haluska of the Oakland
       County Prosecutors office.  They state
       they have all the credentials in from
       the expert in Maryland and are
       determining whether to hire her or not.
       Halushka stated he believes they will.
       Apparently the expense is quite high.

       Halushaka states they are going to wait
       for all lab results are in before
       making a warrant decision which will be
       13 business days from today at the
       most.

       David Schultz
       Traffic Safety Officer
```

Two weeks after the NMS tests come back positive, the prosecutors office is still trying to decide whether to hire an expert from Maryland who deals in the behavior of people on drugs.

    They wanted an open and shut case if they were going to try it.

    At one point they said something about running out of money -- the third richest county on the country. They said they didn't have enough money to fly out there and interview the woman in Maryland.

Patterson happened to run into Gorcyca a couple of days after that and told him the City of Birmingham had money and we would pay for the trip. We'd send one of their people and me.

Patterson told me about it and I was excited -- even though I'm a white-knuckled flyer. But we never heard from them again on that.

Finally, Halushka calls me up and asks me to bring the case up to them. I tell him I'll be in their office at 10 o'clock the next morning.

I walked in that morning and say: "I'm Dave Schultz from Birmingham," and the receptionist tells me to have a seat. And I sit there about 45 minutes before a warrant writer named Jennifer Stout comes out. She takes me back and we sit down and she goes: "Let me take a look at this."

And I tell her I talked to Pernick and Halushka and everybody else on this. I knew I wasn't going to get a warrant on this day, but they just wanted me to bring it up and present it. But she said I had to wait around, "in case I have any questions."

So I sit there and she starts reading the report and every now and then she goes and asks somebody a question, then it comes time for lunch and she tells me she is leaving but I have to be back there in half an hour.

After lunch she looks at the reports a little more and still hasn't really asked me any questions when she gets up and says: "OK, I've got to talk to my bosses."

And I sit there almost three hours. I know something definitely is not right now. This isn't the way business is usually done. Every now and then I pick up a phone and call around trying to find her. I've got things to do and I'm just sitting here. But I'm more upset about why am I not sitting there talking to people about this case?

Around 4 o'clock she comes down and says they're going to further the case, which means they want to look into it some more.

The next day, I'm on the phone with Pridmore, talking about the case and he says: "Hey, where were you yesterday?"

And I ask him what he means.

"Well, we all discussed the case yesterday, Gorcyca and all of his people. And quite frankly I was surprised that the investigating officer wasn't there."

"I was there" I said.

"What do you mean?"

"I was sitting downstairs cooling my heels all day."

I don't know if there was a problem or what, but that isn't the way we're usually treated over there and the discussion we got from them after that was nil.

A lot of time passes and I'm just finishing up a few little things. Basically, I've talked to everybody I think I have to talk to and I keep thinking we'll get something here from the prosecutors office in the next few days. I think I've made my case and the only thing that had to come up now is whether the prosecutors office was going to do anything about it.

Every now and then Deputy Chief Patterson would ask me what was going on and I'd call and they'd say: "We're waiting."

Finally, in late September, I do get a call from Jason Pernick.

He was kind of brusk.

He asked me: "Is there anything else you have to do on this?"

And I said: "No." And I started basically reviewing the case. I said, "we've got this," and "I don't think we need anything else on that unless you can think of something," and he just cuts me off.

"I don't have time to go over this," he says. "I just need to know if you have anything else."

I said: "Well, no."

And he said "OK" and hung up.

The next day they called and said to come up to the prosecutors office, that they would have the warrant ready, that they were going to issue it for suspended license.

That was all. Suspended license.

"What about the driving? We all knew that suspended license was there, that was given from the beginning. But it didn't cause the accident."

What I was trying to say was that just the use of marijuana was illegal.

A case could be made that what he did constituted willful and wanton disregard for the safety of others. I mean, you take a job as a chauffeur, A number one, knowing your not supposed to drive in the first place, because your license is suspended, and number two, ingest an illegal substance in your body that day...he smoked just before he drove. Doing that puts the willful and wanton disregard in there. That's where I was coming from.

I'm basically saying they should charge him with something, but it wasn't even an argument at that point; they just didn't want to hear it. It was just them saying this is what we're going to do and that's it and we're having a press conference at 3 o'clock. You don't have to be there, but if you guys want to, you're invited.

Now it's like 9 a.m. and they're going to have this

press conference six hours later and quite frankly, I'm pissed.

I'm pissed for two reasons: Number one, I thought there should be a different charge, and Number two, nobody has discussed it with me.

I put a lot of work into this and I didn't think the explanations I had gotten to that point were grounds for not charging the guy. The guy caused the accident. Or at least he should be made available to a jury to determine if they thought that.

But they didn't want to talk to me, so I went to Patterson's office and told him about it and brought up the part about the driving and he said: "I agree with you."

So Patterson called our attorneys, Dan Christ and Tim Currier, at the law firm of Beier, Howlett, who our city has used for a long time and they tell him to send me over to talk to them.

Their offices are at Long Lake and Woodward and I shoot up there, with my whole file in a big black book, with the same copies the prosecutors office has and I sit down with them and give them a brief resume of what happened and they both couldn't understand why he wasn't being charged.

They said: "There has to be more; tell us the bad part."

I told 'em I was telling 'em everything.

We decided to meet back at the police department a little before noon.

What we were starting to think at this point is that our city attorneys might make the charges against him. We're looking at an accident, we're the City of Birmingham, we're the police department, we've investigated something. There's a crime here and it has happened before that the prosecutors office didn't want a case and we'd handle it through the city attorney's office.

So we all get together in Patterson's office, go over some stuff again and Christ says he believes Gnida should be charged with driving under the influence of narcotics and causing a serious injury. We can't charge felonies, but what we can do is charge him with driving under the influence of narcotics and that would be the ultimate slap at the prosecutors office. But we were leaning more towards reckless driving.

All this time -- since I talked to the prosecutors office before 9 o'clock -- they don't know up there that we've been having these meetings and basically, considering what we can do.

So Patterson calls them and says we need to talk about this, that we have a problem.

At first, he's talking mostly to Halushka and now Halushka is attempting to give us some sort of explanation of their thinking. We just kind of went back and forth and obviously weren't making any progress so Patterson said to them: "Get all your people together and we'll have a conference call at 1 o'clock and see what we have here."

Between phone calls, I call up the National Medical Services, and talk to Michael Robertson, who signed their report certifying the amount of marijuana in Gnida's system indicated he had smoked marijuana just hours before the accident.

As soon as I identify myself on the phone, Robertson said: "I've been waiting for your subpoena"

"Well," I said, "the prosecutors office is having a hard time."

He seemed kind of shocked at that.

"I want to get this right," I told him. "You'll testify to what it says here on this thing, these are the test results and with your experience, you'll testify that he smoked marijuana within six hours of the accident and possibly as close as three hours?"

"Absolutely."

So I thank him and go into the office for the conference call. When they finally get everyone rounded up on both ends it's about 1:30 -- like 90 minutes before Gorcyca is supposed to have the press conference saying Gnida is going to be charged with only the driving on a suspended license.

On our end, it's Chief Edward Ostin, Deputy Chief Patterson, the two lawyers and myself; on their end, it's Gorcyca, John O'Brian, the chief assistant, Halushka, Pernick and at one time they went out and got John Skrzynski, on of their top-gun prosecutors, and that's when it started going back and forth. Everybody was involved but most of the talking was done by Patterson and by me on our end and by Gorcyca and Halushka on theirs.

I argued that their charge had nothing to do with the accident. I said: "If a guy falls asleep behind the wheel of a vehicle for no reason and goes over a median and kills somebody, you're not going to charge him with something?"

Gorcyca's reply was: "I don't want to go there."

Both the chief and Patterson kind of let me go and the thing got pretty heated at some points, there were some long and loud bouts and it was clear, at some point, that Patterson was more the voice of reason than I was. I realized that and wrote a note to the chief, who was sitting beside me: "Am I being out of line? Should I shut up?"

He shook his head "no" and mouthed that I was

doing fine.

In the course of all this, Halushka says that the problem is they have no one to testify to the connection between smoking and the accident.

"Robertson will testify," I said.

"No. I talked to him," Halushka said, "and he won't come up."

I'm screaming now.

"I talked to him not ten minutes ago on the telephone and he told me that alls he's waiting for is the subpoena."

There was silence on the other end of the line and then the subject got changed. That was it.

From there we just went around and around. We told them that we could charge Gnida with operating under the influence of narcotics or maybe with careless driving. We couldn't as a city, charge him with any felony but charging him with either driving under the influence or

Deputy Chief Deputy Patterson both drove and supported me throughout the investigation (Robert DIckson)

reckless would make the prosecutors office look bad and on their end now, we can tell they were very upset.

Patterson made a point of telling them we were examining our position on this and that we didn't want a war with the prosecutors office but we do have a responsibility and that's when Gorcyca says: "Well, we've got a press conference scheduled for 3 o'clock...if you screw us on this there will be hell to pay."

We're going back and forth over the same ground and Patterson kind of holds his hand up to me, like to say it's time to back off, that we don't need to go over the same things anymore.

He tried to play peacemaker after Gorcyca's threat, but when we hung up it was with the understanding that we were leaving our options open.

We knew, though, what the prosecutors office was going to do for sure.

At 3 o'clock on October 1 -- six hours before the Detroit Red Wings opened the 1997-98 National Hockey League season in Calgary -- Richard Gorcyca said that the Oakland County Prosecutors Office was charging Gnida with driving on a suspended license, second offense, because Dr. Marilyn Heustis of the National Institutes of Health in Maryland could not determine what role, if any, the drug had on causing the crash.

"We cannot conclude," Gorcyca said, "if Gnida's marijuana use inhibited his operation of the limousine that night. Because of that, my hands are legally tied."

CHAPTER 7

I guess I felt sort of defeated.

I'd had a night to sleep on it and I knew what to expect when I came in the next morning.

I knew if we tried to press our position too hard, we would step on a lot of toes and I understood the political ramifications.

The chief calls me in and I knew how it was going to go -- if I was the chief or deputy chief, I would probably make the same decision they did, but just the same I figured they were prepared for me to blow up for a little while. But I didn't.

I knew we, the City of Birmingham, could charge Gnida with careless driving and that's what they'd decided to do; it's a civil infraction, no major court case or anything. But I am still convinced that something else should have happened and I wrote a press release, too, stating that it was my contention that the guy did have marijuana in his system. That was very critical to me, because I kept hearing people say: "If he did have marijuana in his system, the prosecutors office would have charged him."

Patterson and Ostin read my press release and OK'd that and I walked in front of the police station and made a statement that we were going to issue a careless driving charge and that all the evidence shows that Gnida was smoking marijuana that day...as soon as I'm done, everybody is screaming: "Whoa! Whoa! Gorcyca's not saying that!" and I say: "Hey, listen, that's them, this is us."

I was quite surprised. I thought that would fuel some fires, that someone would ask the prosecutors office some more questions, based on that. But it just died.

It was just my belief -- still is -- that this is a person who should be in front of 12 people to decide if he committed the crime or not. That's all I'm saying should have happened. I think we had enough to go before a judge and eventually in front of a jury and say: "This man was driving and A number one, shouldn't have been driving, because he didn't have a license in the first place, went over four lanes of traffic, there's people screaming at him and he still didn't come to until the last second and he swerved and hit a tree."

In the only statement he ever made, he said he must have passed out or must have blacked out. OK. There's witnesses, eye witnesses, who said there was nothing in the roadway. He didn't swerve to avoid anything in the roadway. All indications are that he was unconscious and there was no medical reason we went unconscious. Put on your toxicologist to say this man injested marijuana within hours of getting behind the wheel.

I'm not even saying we should have convicted; I'm saying he should have been charged. The issue is: It's a jury question. It should have been left to them to decide.

That wasn't going to happen, though.

All that's left after Gorcyca's charge and ours, is for Gnida to appear for an arraignment and to determine what happens from there, if he stands mute or pleads one way or the other.

At his arraignment, his attorney doesn't even show up.

That tells me more about the guy, who I already had problems with. I told Gnida that day -- again -- that if he wanted to talk, I would be happy to listen. I told him, if he still felt he had information on Gambino that we would want, that he should talk to us before sentencing, because it might be helpful to him. He said he understood, but I never heard from him about it.

I asked him, that same day, too, because I had a problem with O'Connell, if he had paid his attorney. He told me he hadn't paid him anything but that he thought "a friend of the family" was paying him.

I asked him, too, if he was OK, because generally an attorney is with his client for an arraignment so he can explain anything that might not be clear. But he was there by himself and he stood mute when the judge read the charges. The only other thing was to address the bond and he had no money, so I took him with me up to the county jail.

When I dropped him off, I got hold of the jail people and told them: "Look, this is Richard Gnida, the Red Wing guy, blah, blah, blah and blah, blah, blah...he's not a big guy and there might be some people in there who might want to kick his ass," and they said they would keep an eye on that. They do that kind of thing.

He told me later that they basically isolated him, but he wasn't there long, because I guess his family remortgaged their house and got him out that afternoon; his dad was very ill and died the next day.

The fact that I wasn't pleased with the way the whole thing turned out didn't mean I didn't have sympathy for the guy in a lot of ways.

It wasn't that I wanted to get this guy or anything like that. I mean, he seemed like a nice guy; I don't think there's anyway he wanted to do this...I think he's a very simple, very slow guy, the kind of guy that the first thing friends and family would say about him is: "He'd never hurt a flea."

But that's not the point.

I didn't know if he deserved more than nine months, but he should have been charged with something different.

I didn't feel that I had closure regarding the accident. The story of what caused the accident still wasn't out there and that really bugged me.

On October 20, just over four months after the accident, Gnida plead guilty to driving on a suspended license, before Judge Kimberly Small of the 48th District Court.

O'Connell, explaining why he did not ask for a jury trial, said: "We plead guilty because he was guilty."

What I found ironic was the sentence the judge handed down.

She could have given him a year in jail, but she wanted to add some provisions that would keep him under observation after he was released, so she sentenced him to nine months, but added the provision that he was to attend four Narcotics Anonymous meetings a week until he is off probation.

But the charge was for driving on a suspended license. He wasn't convicted of anything relating to drugs, but the judge added NA meetings as a provision after his jail time.

Do you think that says anything about the real cause of the accident?

Through all of it, though, I never managed to feel any anger or animosity towards Gnida.

After he pleaded guilty, he went to sit down; I'd been right behind him and O'Connell in the courtroom and I said: "Richard, come with me," and I take him back and lock him in the holding cell and come back out, because I've got

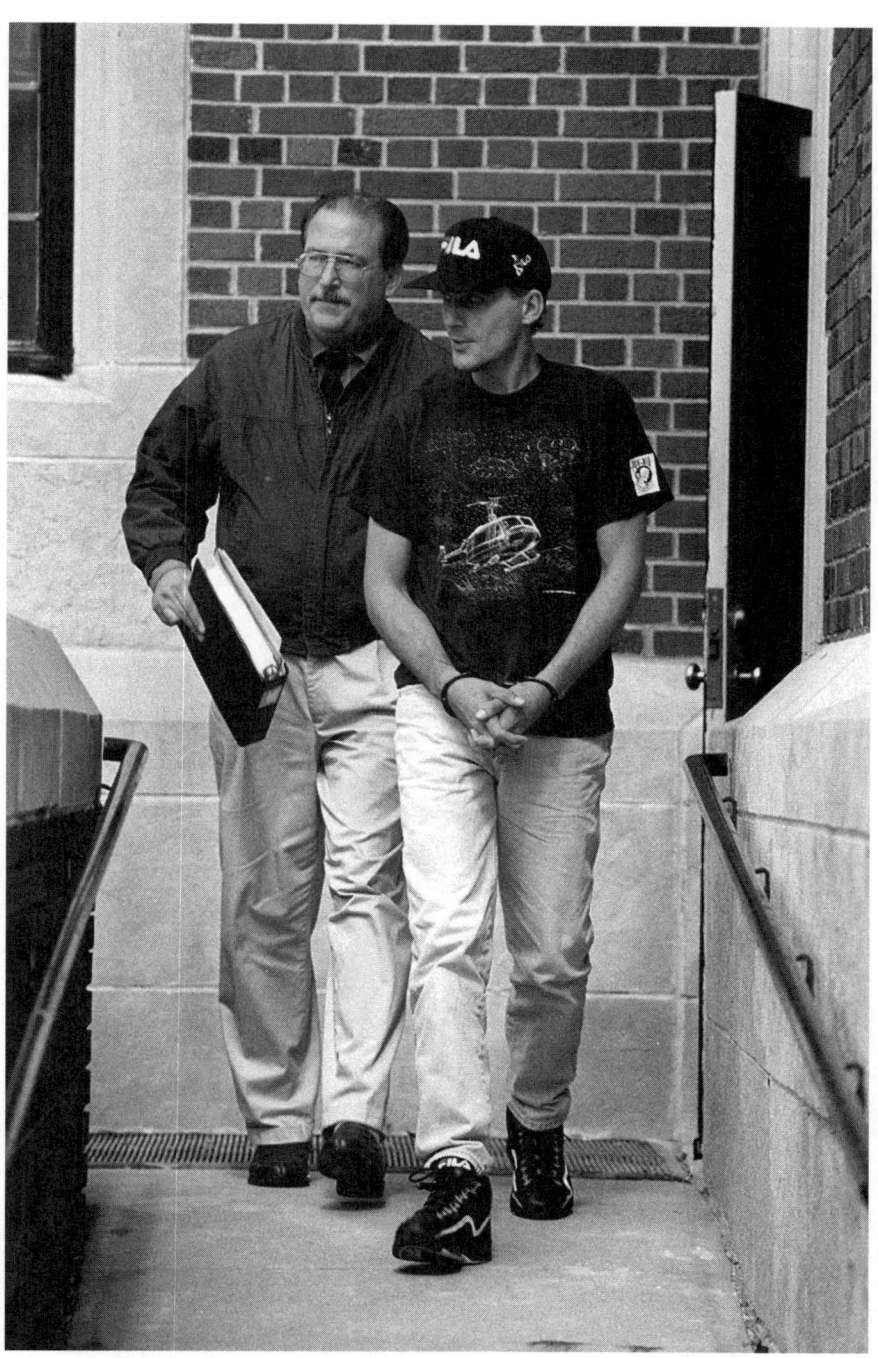

I couldn't feel any anger at Gnida, even when I escorted him to jail on October 2. But he should have been charged with something other than driving on a suspended license, because that isn't what caused the accident. (Mary Schroeder/Detroit Free Press)

about half a hour's worth of paperwork to get ready to commit him.

I do the paper work, get him in the car and drive him up to the county jail and drop him off. It's about a seven or eight mile drive up Telegraph and we talked about things, about Gambino and how he's doing and things like that.

When I got there, I pulled in and take him inside and once you walk in with him, they open up the doors and the doors lock behind you. Then they pat down the prisoner in front of the jailer to make sure he doesn't have anything on him.

Richard knew he was going to jail and didn't have anything. No lighters, nothing.

The door opens to the bullpen, where he stays while they're processing him and we sort of look at each other.

"Thanks for everything," he said.

"You be careful up here," I told him.

He said: "OK," and began a nine month sentence for a crime.

But not the right one.

Good news was hard to come by in the aftermath of the accident, but here's a nice scene: Vladimir Konstantinov (bottom, center) with his Red Wings teammates at the White House with President Clinton in February. (Mary Schroeder/Detroit Free Press)

CHRONOLOGY

Saturday, June 7
Detroit Red Wings complete sweep of Philadelphia Flyers, 2-1, to return the Stanley Cup to Detroit after an absence of 42 years.

Monday, June 9
At a party at Joe Louis Arena, for season ticket holders, suite holders and sponsors, Vladimir Konstantinov draws an enormous ovation after a nine-word speech: "You're the greatest and you deserve it. Thank you."

Tuesday, June 10
An estimated one million people jam downtown Detroit for a parade down Woodward Avenue, honoring the Stanley Cup winners.

Friday, June 13
Returning from a team golf outing at the Orchard Golf Club, a limousine containing Konstantinov, Slava Fetisov and Red Wings masseur Sergei Mnatsakanov veers out of control and hits a tree in the median of Woodward, near 16 mile road in Birmingham at 9:10 p.m. The driver of the limo is 27-year-old Richard Gnida, whose license has been suspended.

Saturday, June 14
Konstantinov and Mnatsakanov are in critical condition at William Beaumont Hospital, both with severe head injuries; Fetisov's most serious injuries are to his chest and lungs.

Monday, June 16
Dave Schultz assumes control of the investigation of the accident; Wreckage of the limo is inspected by Schultz and state trooper Larry Richardson and a drug dog finds no significant evidence of any illegal substance.

Another driver for John Gambino's limousine service is arrested in Birmingham on a warrant for driving with a suspended license.

Tuesday, June 17

Gnida and his attorney, James O'Connell, meet with Schultz. Gnida gives only his name and birthdate before O'Connell informs Schultz his client will say no more.

Blood drawn from Gnida less than two hours after the accident is sent to state laboratory to be tested for drugs.

Wednesday, June 18

Interviewed at Beaumont Hospital, Fetisov says Konstantinov had concerns with Gnida's driving almost from the moment they stepped into the car at Chris Osgood's home Friday afternoon.

Thursday, June 19

The first of the phone calls -- from a Westland waitress -- that make accusations about Gnida's alleged drug use.

State lab notifies Birmingham police that its analysis of Gnida's blood showed no opiates, amphetamines, barbiturates, benzodiazepines, cocaine or a class of drug which includes valium and informs Schultz that it can not analyze samples other than urine for the presence of marijuana.

Friday, June 20

Birmingham Deputy Chief Richard Patterson authorizes the state lab to send one tube of Gnida's blood to the Toxicology Lab Center in Lansing for marijuana testing.

Monday, June 23

Patterson instructs the Lansing lab to also test for LSD; Lab spokesman says it is not qualified to testify in court on LSD presence.

Schultz contacts National Medical Services in Philadelphia to test for LSD, since the Lansing lab would be unable to testify. Blood samples sent to Philadelphia

Tuesday, June 24

Lansing lab says both marijuana and LSD testing were negative. National Medical Services authorized to test blood for marijuana.

Saturday, June 28
Red Wing's trainer John Wharton tells Schultz he has heard that there have been some veiled threats against some of the Red Wings.

Monday, June 30
Schultz notifies Oakland County Prosecutors Office about Wharton's concerns.

Tuesday, July 1
Dr. David Collon, Red Wings' team physician, relays to Schultz information that the Beaumont Hospital public relations staff had received calls about potential incriminating photos. Collon says players, after being contacted, seemed unconcerned. This accusation proves false.

Thursday, July 3
Steve Facione, vice president of Olympia Entertainment tells Schultz that two secretaries employed by Olympia Entertainment, owner of the Red Wings, had received phone calls that could be categorized as threatening and one of the callers said: "I tried to warn you in the letter."

National Medical Services reports no LSD in Gnida's blood.

Saturday, July 5
Schultz begins interviewing other drivers who transported the Red Wings on June 13.

Monday, July 7
Schultz meets with FBI special agent Charles Whistler to discuss the possibility of Russian Mafia involvement in the accident.

Tuesday, July 8
Whistler faxes to Schultz newspaper stories of the murder of Russian hockey president, Valentin Sych.

Wednesday, July 9
With Harold Paulson, Schultz searches the limo in an attempt to find a cellular phone number for the car; instead, they discover a partially smoked cigarette that appears to contain marijuana.

Schultz authorizes National Medical Services to screen for psychedelic drugs and a new drug "used to induce sound sleep," and forwards the cigarette found in the limo for testing.

Thursday, July 10

Attorney James O'Connell tells Schultz that Gnida can provide evidence John Gambino knew Gnida's license was suspended.

Monday, July 14

After being asked by Oakland County Prosecutors office to present it with his files, Schultz calls National Medical Services for final drug results and is told Gnida's blood sample has tested positive for marijuana.

Thursday, July 17

Facione and Olympia's security chief, Tim Sopha, tell Schultz there have been no more telephone calls implying threats and that research turns up no evidence that the Red Wings received any threatening letter prior to the accident.

Oakland County Chief Toxicologist, Phil Pridmore, asks Schultz to release information on drug testing to his office, after NMS refused to acknowledge for Pridmore that it has run Gnida's tests.

Monday, July 21

NMS confirms the partially smoked cigarette found July 9 is marijuana.

Attorney, O'Connell again advises that Gnida wants to talk with him but O'Connell says timing my be a problem, since he tentatively has a murder trial, beginning July 22.

Tuesday, July 22

Oakland County assistant prosecutor Jim Haluska says his office is consulting with an independent source in Maryland about the NMS findings.

NMS advises that the screen for one of the suspected "Russian" drugs is negative.

Wednesday, July 23
Stephen R. Syson-Hille and Associates of Goleta, California, inspects limousine on behalf of Konstantinov's interests.

Friday, July 25
Dennis Lark, Sye Linovitz and Timothy Kmiec of Ford Motor Company inspect the limousine.

Monday, July 28
O'Connell contacts Schultz to say Gnida no longer wants to talk with Birmingham police.

Tuesday, August 5
NMS reports Gnida's blood shows no traces of the second and last "Russian" drug.

Friday, August 15
Cellmark Diagnostics notifies Schultz that DNA on the marijuana cigarette butt does not match Gnida's.

Wednesday, October 1
Prosecutor David Gorcyca announces Oakland County's only charge against Gnida will be for driving with a suspended license, second offense.

Thursday, October 2
City of Birmingham charges Gnida with careless driving.

Monday, October 20
Richard Gnida pleads guilty to driving with a suspended license and is sentenced to nine months in Oakland County jail, followed by mandatory Narcotics Anonymous meetings.

ACKNOWLEDGEMENTS

I want to thank all the people who assisted in the planning, production and the encouragement in writing of this book.

Special Thanks to:

> Chief Ed Ostin, whose leadership I have followed for 21 years. A special prayer for his lovely wife, Sharon.
>
> Deputy Chief Richard Patterson for his support during the investigation.
>
> Commander Donald Studt for his keen legal mind, encouragement and longtime friendship.
>
> Ellen DeView and Debbie Fitzpatrick of the Police Services Division for their invaluable technical support during the investigation.
>
> All the men and women of the Birmingham Police Department for your dedication and professionalism.
>
> Don Canham, a man I have long admired, for his ideas and technical assistance.
>
> The Detroit Free Press, especially Gene Myers, Dave Robinson and Rob Kozloff, for graciously allowing the use of its photos and front page reproductions.
>
> Tom Strech for the book title idea.
>
> Tom Stevens for listening.
>
> Charlie Vincent, an honorable and talented man, who made a dream come true.
>
> My wife, Kathy, for being there.

Dave Schultz
April 1998

DISCLAIMER

The facts and information contained in this book are based largely on public records, the author's investigation, and on conversastions in which the author participated. The opinions and representations of the author contained herein and the conclusions which he has drawn therefrom are solely the opinions, representations, and conclusions of the author. They do not necessarily reflect the opinions and/or conclusion of the City of Birmingham or its Police Department. No representation is hereby made by this book, nor should any be implied, that the City of Birmingham or its Police Department agrees with or in any way endorses the opinions contained in this book or expresses any opinion as to the accuracy of the representations and conclusions contained herein, and the City of Birmingham assumes no responsibility for the contents or accuracy of this book or for the statements and opinions expressed herein.

Dave Schultz, 42, has spent half of his life on the Birmingham Police Department, working in juvenile division, undercover narcotics and traffic, twice being named Birmingham's Police Officer of the Year; Charlie Vincent (right) is 58 and has been with the Detroit Free Press since January of 1970. In 1981, 1989, and 1992 he was named among the top five sports columnists in the United States. His previous book, Welcome to My World, was a collection of his columns from the Detroit Free Press (Robert Dickson)